The Secret to Being a Good Therapist

Looking after Yourself whilst
Looking after Others

DEBORAH LLOYD

Hyp Dip, GQHP, LHS, MFHT

The information contained in this book recommends to always inform your health care professional before starting any complementary or additional treatments or therapies or when making major changes in your diet or exercise programme.

The recommendations in this book are to be used as a complementary therapy to conventional medicine, as it complements any medical treatment or medication, the client may be taking.

Every client is asked to continue any medication they may be taking and is always recommended to consult their health care professional for advice, diagnosis, and treatment. We are not allowed by law to diagnose or to claim a 'cure', and there are no guarantees that the recommendations in this book will work for everyone.

Copyright © All rights reserved.

No part of this book may be reproduced by any means or to be stored electronically or photographically for either private or public use, without the express written consent of the author.

ISBN: 9781728823850

Cover design by Deborah Lloyd /
Chris Emery Cwench
Graphics by Emma Paxton Imagistic

DEDICATION

To my husband, Kev, who has supported me throughout my holistic journey. You have been the most willing mind, body, and spirit for me to work with.

Thank you, darling, I could not have done it without you.

FOREWORD

I have known Deborah in a professional capacity for several years, and I have always found her warm and engaging. This book has combined these traits with her years of practical experience.

The result is an easy to read, and a very useful book for complementary therapists across the spectrum, particularly for those just starting out.

I would highly recommend all therapists read this book. Even after 15 years of working as a self-employed chiropractor running my own business, there were still several points that gave me cause to reflect.

Lee Ayres
M(chiro), BSc (Hons)

x

ACKNOWLEDGEMENTS

I would like to say thank you to the staff at Swindon College. My friends and colleagues in the IT Department and the tutors and students in the Hair and Beauty Department.

Thank you to Remo for his encouragement, inspiration, and support.

Thank you to Charlie, who opened my eyes not only to the world of holistic therapy but to life itself.

A thank you to my dear friend Sandra for your immense love and support.

A special thank you to mum and dad for choosing me.

Thank you to all the tutors and students that helped me on my holistic journey. There are far too many of you to mention, but you know who you are.

CONTENTS

FOREWORD IX
ACKNOWLEDGEMENTS XI
WHO SHOULD READ THIS? 19
MY JOURNEY SO FAR 23
KNOW YOUR GOAL 27
THE FIRST CONTACT 35
LOCATION, LOCATION, LOCATION 39
MEET AND GREET 43
INITIAL CONSULTATION 47
CONSULTATION FORMS 50
FIRST IMPRESSION 51
SETTING THE GROUND RULES 55
PICTURES AND SMELLS 57
ROOM ETIQUETTE 61
MINIMISING INTERRUPTIONS 65
EQUIPMENT AND STOCK 67
APPOINTMENTS 75
TIMEKEEPING 83
CONFIDENTIALITY 85
KNOWING WHEN TO SHUT UP 87
MALE THERAPISTS 89
BECOME AN EXPERT 90
PRICE INCREASES 97

DISCOUNTING	99
LOYALTY SCHEMES	105
REFERRALS	107
DISCOUNT VOUCHER SCHEMES	109
GIFT VOUCHERS	113
POLICIES, TERMS AND CONDITIONS	117
QUALIFICATIONS	119
INSURANCE	120
DRUGS	125
PAY ATTENTION	129
TIME IS MONEY	131
CLIENTS TELLING YOU WHAT TO DO	133
I AM SO BUSY!	137
I MUST GO	138
COLDS AND FLU	139
RENTING A ROOM	141
WORKING IN A SALON	144
VOLUNTEERING	149
WORKING FROM HOME	153
WORKING ONLINE	157
MOBILE THERAPY	163
WORKING WITH THE NATIONAL HEALTH SERVICE (NHS)	164
WORKING WITH FAMILIES	165
WORKING WITH CHILDREN	167
ABREACTIONS	169
CONTACT INFORMATION	172

DIARY MANAGEMENT	175
THIRD-PARTY SOFTWARE	177
AFTERCARE	179
NOTE TAKING	181
GIFTS FROM CLIENTS	185
COMPLAINTS	187
MARKETING	189
BRANDING	195
ADVERTISING	196
WHERE TO ADVERTISE	199
WHO IS YOUR IDEAL CLIENT?	213
GIVEAWAYS	214
SOCIAL MEDIA	217
FAIRS	221
NETWORKING	229
WORKSHOPS	239
GIVING PRESENTATIONS	240
WALK THE TALK	245
SECURITY	249
LADIES/GENTS WHO LATTE	255
WORKING HOURS	256
HEALTH AND SAFETY	257
THINGS TO CLAIM FOR	266
ACCOUNTANT	275
TAX FORMS	276
CONTINUOUS PROFESSIONAL DEVELOPMENT (CPD)	279

TESTIMONIALS	285
BEING A CONFIDENT MASSEUSE	289
COLOUR THERAPY	293
PREGNANCY	295
CHAKRAS	297
BREATHING	299
CRYSTALS	303
HEALING	307
AFFIRMATIONS	309
ESSENTIAL OILS	311
ABOUT THE AUTHOR	314
CONTACT DEBORAH	315

PART ONE

SETTING UP YOUR BUSINESS

WHO SHOULD READ THIS?

The Secret to Being a Good Therapist is the go-to book for the student, recently qualified and experienced therapists.

I have many years' experience of working as a holistic therapist. Before that, I had a varied background working in retail, sales, and marketing, financial services, and personnel. As a result, I was able to draw on my many experiences to help me be successful. It was as reflected on my path to date that I came to realize that there are some great therapists, but they don't all know how to run a business.

Many people have said to me "I wasn't taught how to run a business at college".

I have written this book to help you on your journey. You have probably invested a lot of time, money, and effort to pass your course(s) and now don't know where to start.

This book is suitable for chiropractors, physiotherapists, holistic therapists, hypnotherapists, counsellors, and beauticians.

In other words, anyone who wants to provide a health and wellbeing service.

As most therapists are women, I have written this book from a woman's point of view. However, a lot of it is still relevant to male therapists.

I structured this book in sections so that you can either read it as a whole or dip in and out to find relevant information. However, there is much overlap in some of the topics.

There are also plenty of pages for you to write your own notes and ideas.

I wish you every success in your professional career.

MY JOURNEY SO FAR ……

I have worked for many corporate companies in IT departments. I worked hard, played hard, and I didn't eat well. I also drank and smoked too much. I was in a toxic relationship, and I worked 13-hour days, six days a week.

When cutbacks where being made, the IT departments were hit hardest, and I went through a phase of repeatedly being made redundant. When I started working at Swindon College, my boss, the IT Director, told me I could have free treatments downstairs in the Hair and Beauty department. He said it was a "perk" of the job, yet my reaction was initially dismissive. What? Is he mad? Why would I want that? Plus, I thought I didn't have the time, so I carried on typing away at my computer.

After a year, I got to know all the tutors and the returning students. So, in May, when they were crying out for "bodies" to work on, I said I'd help. I returned to the IT suite, to the mostly male team I worked with and said: "Come on guys we need to help our students".

And so, began our weekly massages, pedicures, and reflexology. I used to smile when, a few weeks later, some of the guys would ask me what time their facial was that week!

One of the tutors laughed at me and said: "You will be learning this!" My reply was "No way, I only like receiving, not giving" (how naive and selfish). The same tutor also recommended I buy a book. It was my first holistic book - The Little Blue Book by Louise Hay.

Then, one day I received an Indian Head Massage from a superb student called Charlie. It completely blew me away, and I knew then that my life would have to change. I remember thinking wow if something like this is so powerful, I need to learn it. And so, my holistic journey began!

KNOW YOUR GOAL

There are many tried and tested therapies that have been around for many years. Some have even been around for centuries. People know of them, slightly understand them, and may know the benefits.

When you learn any therapy, you will discover a new thirst for knowledge, and you will want to learn, learn, learn. I believe this curiosity is a double-edged sword. It will add to your list of therapies, but it can lead to distraction and a loss of focus. I recommend that you concentrate on what the type of treatment you are providing and make sure that it is what you want to be known for.

My first diploma was in Indian head massage, followed by aromatherapy; reflexology; Swedish body massage; and ear candles.

I stayed with bodywork but found I was getting upset by absorbing people's problems, so I trained in counselling. I would highly recommend that all therapists take a counselling course. It helps you set boundaries, understand about transference and a whole host of other things, not just about your clients, but also about you.

Later, I concentrated on spiritual work: Reiki; Munay Ki; shamanic healing; runes; tarot; and working with crystals.

I had always believed in the power of the mind. I think it was because I attended my first hypnotherapy workshop 20 years before starting my holistic training. I knew in my heart that is what I wanted to be.

Eventually, I reached the point in my holistic career where I was regularly referring clients on to a local hypnotherapist. It was then that I realized that it was now time to learn to be a hypnotherapist myself.

I took courses in hypnotherapy, eye movement desensitization and reprocessing (EMDR), advanced post-traumatic stress disorder (PTSD), and inner child therapy.

Today, I feel blessed that I have followed this path. All these things are working with the client holistically, which means working with the mind, body, and spirit. The reason I am telling you this is so you can remember to follow your path. As I said before, we can sometimes get diverted. Therapists have a thirst for learning. We want to know about the latest, sometimes fad, therapy. It is a beautiful progression to evolve and move with the times, but it's all too easy to lose your way a little.

Know who YOU are, and that way, you can focus your attention on your chosen role. If you do not know who you are, neither will your client. That said, I know some highly successful therapists who run two different professions in parallel but keep them separate.

For example, you may start as a reflexologist and later tie this in with podiatry. If you are a sports masseur, you may choose to offer manual lymphatic drainage (MLD).

The same goes for your website and price list. Know when you have progressed and when to let things go. What was popular ten years ago may not be now, so delete it off your site and focus on what is popular now or retrain if necessary.

What fits in with your business? I followed a holistic therapy path. I did think about being a nail technician, but it did not fit in with my business plan. I also thought about sports and remedial massage. Again, I refocused on holistic therapy.

Consider additional revenue streams with care. A beautician selling the skincare products they use is great, but a counsellor selling life insurance to their clients is not in line with their business. Decide what fits in with your business, what you need to let go of, and what you would like to train in, to progress.

Always question the course you are about to book. How will it tie in with what you already offer? In my opinion, too many therapists end up offering a great long list of therapies, some holistic, some beauty, some bizarre. If they had stopped to consider how potential clients perceive this lack of specialization, they might have made different choices. You know the old phrase "Jack of all trades, master of none? It can look like you do not know who you are and in what you specialize.

There are always going to be new courses coming along. Figure out whether spending £3000 on a course for a therapy you can only charge £30 for is worth it. In this example, when you do the math's, you will see that you'll need 100 clients to cover the cost of your course before you even start to make a profit. Focus on who you are and what you offer.

Having said all this, it is still a good idea to keep up with the latest trends, so you know what people are talking about if they call you for it.

Notes and Ideas

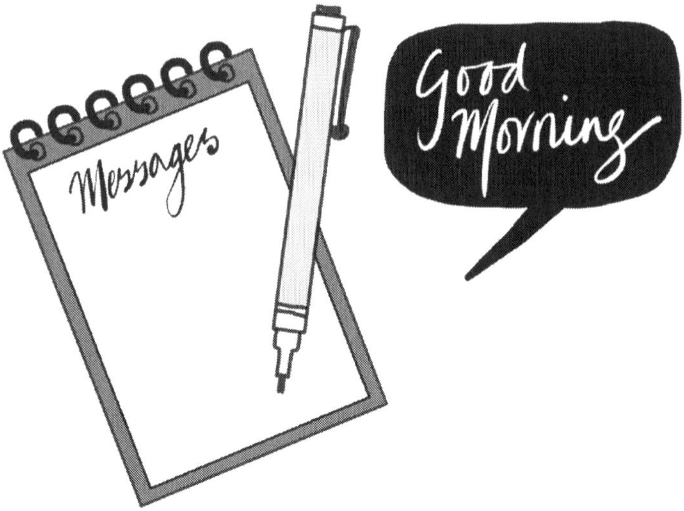
Messages
Good Morning

THE FIRST CONTACT

Have a notepad and pen by your telephone. If you are working from home, ensure everyone in your household answers the phone with "good morning/afternoon" and your business name. They can then take a message if you are busy.

Do have an answerphone with a clear message that states:

- Your name
- Your business name
- A request for them to leave a name and number so that that you can call them back

These days I find that many of my clients prefer to use either email or social media messenger as the first point of contact.

Your website and social media pages should have a contact form which will automatically reply to any client enquiry. This tells the potential client that you have received their message and that you will be in contact soon.

Time-saving tip:
I find that many people ask the same things. So, I have created a series of timesaving, standard reply email templates for regular questions.

Notes and Ideas

DIRECTIONS

75 GREEN CRESCENT
CROSS TOWN. TB75 3PB

PLEASE PARK ON THE DRIVE.

LOCATION, LOCATION, LOCATION

Make it easy for your clients to find you. Most people have satnavs or Google Maps on their smart mobiles, but some may not. Give them easy directions and allow extra time on their first appointment for them to find you. Let them know where to park and if you have easy access.

If you work from home, make sure you do not upset the neighbours. Make sure your terms and conditions contain a request that visiting clients are to park responsibly and not to turn around in or block your neighbours drives.

If you see them doing this, ask them politely to refrain from doing so as your neighbour has been upset with you (even if they haven't).

Don't underestimate the power of disgruntled neighbours:
I knew of a professional hairdresser who worked from her home, where she had installed a beautiful, purpose-built, salon. Unfortunately, she lived in a cul-de-sac, and her neighbours reported her to the local council because of the traffic her business was generating. Sadly, she had to close her business.

Notes and Ideas

MEET AND GREET

Your client is paying to come and see you. Yes, they are paying for services, and they expect good therapy and quality, but ultimately, they are buying from YOU.

People buy people. So, the people who come to you, feel happy to see you and comfortable with the service you provide. When they stop enjoying the experience, they stop paying. Every time they come for their appointment, welcome them as if it were the very first time. Greet them with a warm smile and a sincere "how are you?" After every session, say how lovely it was to see them again and thank them for coming.

Before starting the therapy session, follow up on what was troubling your client on the previous visit and ask if it is still bothering them. Listen carefully to the response. Focus on them exclusively and make them feel special.

If sounds obvious, but when you have been seeing the same clients for years, you can get complacent. It's easy to start moaning about your problems, rather than concentrating on theirs. If you expect your clients to carry on coming, just to listen to you, then you are wrong. They will soon find someone else who makes them feel special, and you will lose their repeat business.

Notes and Ideas

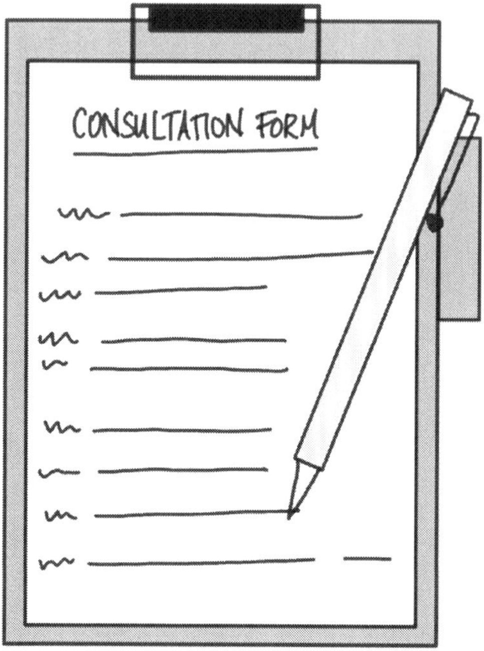
CONSULTATION FORM

INITIAL CONSULTATION

Remember to spend extra time with your clients on the initial consultation so that you can gather relevant information and build trust and rapport with your client.

Listen carefully to identify their needs.

- What are they coming for?
- What are they hoping to achieve?
- What made them come now?

In the UK, doctors' appointments typically last just 12 minutes, so it's no wonder that patients often feel rushed, ignored, and misunderstood. Give your clients what they need on the first appointment by giving them extra time. Being made the focus of attention and listened to without interruption is a prestigious but rare experience for most people. They may even tell you that they have never been heard in this way before. After that, you can stick to your tight appointment times in future sessions.

In my experience, some clients know what they want and book in for a specific treatment. You may find, after the initial consultation, that you feel an alternative approach would be better than the one they have booked. Such a recommendation can be risky on the first visit, especially if it involves an additional fee. If they have booked in for one therapy and receive another, you run the risk of them not liking it.

I recommend that you always give them what they came for initially, and then suggest they may benefit from the other therapy next time.

Marketing Tip:
Always ask new clients how they found you and what made them choose your business. Capturing this sort of information will help you with your marketing. It'll tell you which advertising media or online channels are most effective for your business. If it were a personal referral, you could thank the referrer, thereby encouraging them to do so again.

CONSULTATION FORMS

I spend years changing and tweaking my consultation forms. If you are offering a variety of therapies, you could use the same format but slightly vary the form fields to capture the required information.

You can download one of mine here.

https://www.thespiritwithin.co.uk/the-secret-to-being-a-good-therapist-book/

Consultation Form

FIRST IMPRESSION

Remember - you don't get a second chance to make a first impression. Your appearance speaks volumes to your clients, so keep your uniform or dress smart and pressed, shoes polished and hair clean and tidy. Hands should be clean and nails nicely manicured. If you have just had lunch, either clean your teeth or have a breath mint. Keep to either no perfume/aftershave, or an exceptionally light one. Some clients can be allergic to certain smells.

Check your uniform or dress regularly. Has it become stained from oils or wax? Do your whites look white or a faded over-washed grey? Does your business polo shirt, the one with your branding on it, look faded? If so, replace it.

Tax Tip:
You may be able to claim tax relief on having your uniform cleaned or repaired. Look online to see if you are eligible https://www.gov.uk

NOTES AND IDEAS

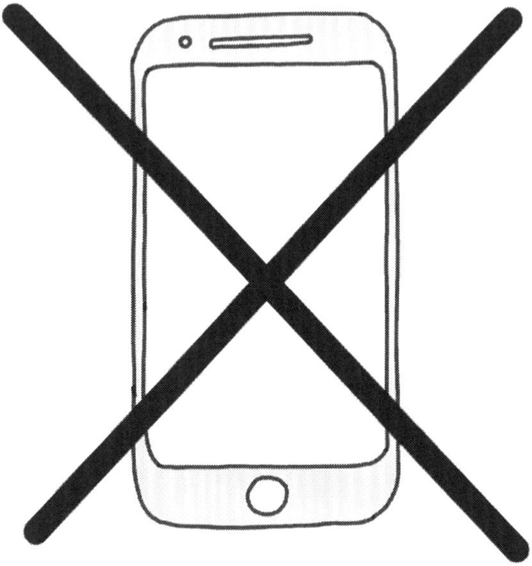

SETTING THE GROUND RULES

I ask my clients to remove their shoes at the door and place them in a box. Doing so helps them to relax, and it also keeps my carpets clean.

I always ask them to switch off their mobile phone rather than just switch it to silent. I explain that this will allow them to relax without being disturbed or distracted by the buzz if it were to vibrate.

I also ask them to remove their watch, reminding them that they are here to relax, not clock watch. I will time keep for them.

You only have to do this once at the initial consultation, and this will set up your expectations for future sessions.

One difficulty you can sometimes encounter is expecting your clients to be clean. We all hope that our clients will have showered before coming for a massage or arrive with clean feet if they have booked reflexology.

I had a client who was a builder. One time he arrived for a treatment having come straight from work on the building site. He was covered in mud, and I did not want him sitting in my therapy chair, let alone being on my clean couch!

I explained that I was unable to massage him today as he was not clean. I offered him Reiki instead, which he accepted and I "hovered over" instead of proving "hands-on". I also put couch roll over the couch and pillow before asking him to lie down. He got the message for next time!

PICTURES AND SMELLS

Be careful of the scents you use in your therapy room. You may like the smell of incense and find sage cleansing, but a chronic asthmatic will not.

Find out, during the initial consultation, what smells your clients like or dislike. A smell like lavender could evoke a beautiful memory of a kind, loving nanny who gave your client lots of love and attention. The same smell, for another client, could evoke memories of a wicked grandmother who beat and tortured her. Fragrances are the quickest way to trigger a memory via the olfactory bulb.

The same goes for decoration. Keep your room neutral and unfussy. You may love angels, but your client may not. A cluttered room means a cluttered mind. Your client may have come to clear their mind, to have some pamper time, and relax.

I once had an Indian Head Massage from a student, and the smell of her hands was disgusting. Instead of relaxing, I ended up holding my breath during the therapy! I told her afterwards that her hands smelt, and it was very off-putting. In reply, she explained that she worked in a fishmonger, and it was the smell of the fish - Ugh!

If you smoke, cigarette smoke clings to every part of you. Either quit smoking or keep your cigarettes until the end of the day when you have finished work. You will not smell it, but your clients will!

Pictures can also trigger memories for your clients. I had a photograph of Burnham Beeches on my wall. I used to play there as a child. It was a beautiful woodland photograph with the sun streaming through the leaves of the trees.

One day I noticed that my client was fidgeting and was staring straight past me at the photograph. When I enquired what was wrong, she told me she had been in a severe car crash in a wood.

A van had hit her sports car so hard the impact flipped the car and shot her into the trees. I removed the photograph straight away, and for every one of her subsequent appointments. After that, I purchased another photo of a beach so that I can alternate them. That incident taught me that a photograph that was someone's representation of relaxation could be another's torment.

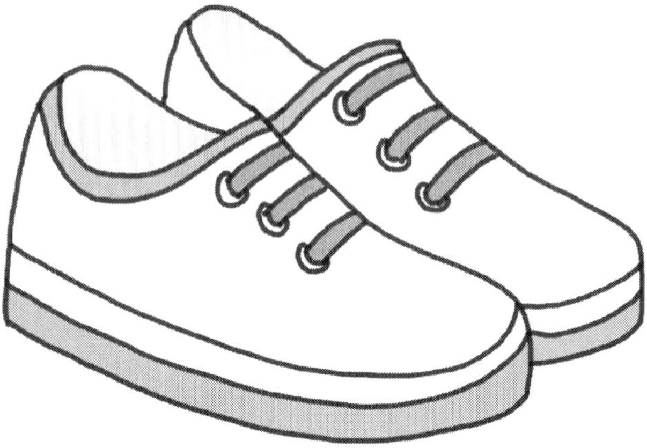

ROOM ETIQUETTE

Unless the client has a parent or guardian, they are the only person I have in my therapy room. As I explained earlier, I request that they remove their coat and shoes in the hall and that they turn off their mobile phone so that they are not disturbed.

I have had clients who wanted to keep their shoes on. When that happens, I am always polite but firm. I say well I would prefer you take them off and I do not let them in the room until they do so. Remember, you are the boss; you make the rules.

I only request this on the initial consultation to set the ground rules. If they leave their mobile phone on for future appointments and the ringing upsets their relaxation, they will not do it again.

Always keep your room clean and tidy for each client. This is especially important for fast turnaround, back to back clients. Allow some space in your diary for a changeover. Clients do not want to come for their appointment and then wait while you make a drink or go to the bathroom.

Check your room from time to time. I walk out of my room and enter it and look at it as if I were seeing it for the first time. When you do this, what do you notice? If you see lots of clutter, have a clear out.

Does your room look tired and in need of decorating? Does the carpet look clean? Is your couch torn?

In the interests of hygiene, please remember to clean your door handles regularly. This is easy to overlook and, if you are working with creams and oils, they very quickly get messy. Clean them after each client using antibacterial wipes to keep germs at bay.

Notes and Ideas

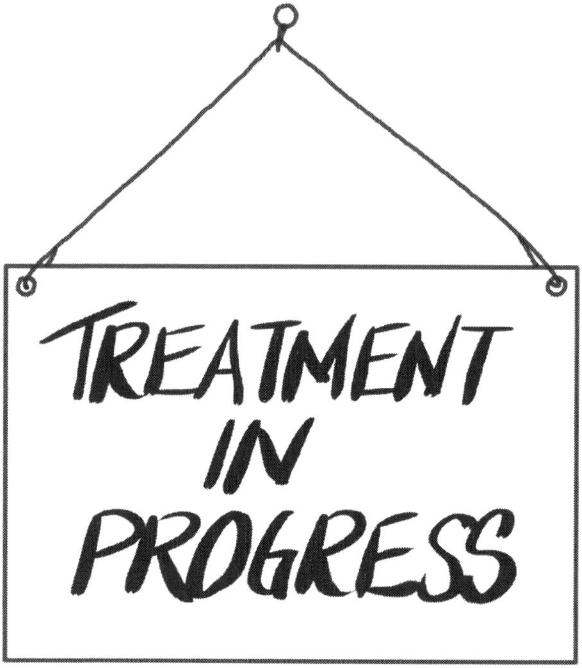
TREATMENT
IN
PROGRESS

MINIMISING INTERRUPTIONS

If you work in a spa or a rented room, you may have an engaged sign on the door. Alternatively, you may have a receptionist that knows when you are with a client and who will stop anyone entering. If you work from home, on the other hand, you may not have this luxury.

I work from home, so I put a sign on my doorstep saying "Treatment in Progress Please do not knock. Thank you." to prevent interruptions.

This approach is also handy for those clients who turn up 20 minutes early, thinking that they will get an extra-long session. Pop your sign out and open the door only at their allocated time.

EQUIPMENT AND STOCK

Couch

When you are starting, it's hard to invest a lot of money on your equipment. Consider it a bit like buying your first home, build up to it gradually. The tips in this section will save you from making expensive purchasing mistakes.

My first couch was a portable model. These are slim, lightweight, and ideal for taking to wellbeing fairs or using for mobile work. However, I wanted something more permanent and comfortable in my practice.

One day I was driving past a local hospital, and I saw a treatment bed dumped outside. I went inside, asked if I could have it, and they said yes. They were getting rid of it because one of the wheels did not turn, which was not a problem for me.

It was a hydraulic bed, which meant it was raised and lowered using a pump-action foot pedal. This was great until I had to massage a twenty stone man. I did, however, keep it for years, and it served me well.

Later, I invested in an electric couch, and I have never looked back. I bought an extra-wide model with extra padding and a separate head and arm cradle. I still use it today, so it was while worth the investment.

Never underestimate the value of a comfortable couch! I recently had a massage in a salon, and because it was narrow, my arms kept falling off the edge of the table. It is not very relaxing when you are just dozing off, and your arms suddenly drop towards the floor. Worse still is that you cannot relax because you are trying to keep your arms on.

The answer is, buy the best you can afford. If you can afford the electric couch straight away, your clients and your back will love you for it.

Couch cover

Toweling covers can hold oils and can quickly become stained, especially if you buy a light colour like lilac. A more luxurious option is velour. I recommend choosing a dark colour, such as emerald or grey.

Couch Roll

While paper couch roll may seem like an excellent way to save on washing your couch covers; they are not much fun for the well-oiled client that is stuck to it when you ask them to roll over. Invariably, they will take the couch roll with them and end up on your cover anyway.

If you have a head cradle, fleece covers fit well, and if you want to save on washing, you can purchase disposable face cradle covers. These work well. I don't recommend using couch roll on your head cradle as your client will either inhale it or eat it!

Towels

Purchase these from a wholesaler, and you can get reasonable quality ones on a budget. You want them to last and not go stringy. Also, you want them to feel soft. There is nothing worse than having crunchy towels next to your skin, so make sure you tumble dry them after washing them. Consider purchasing dark coloured towels, especially if you are using a lot of essentials oils. Light coloured ones will discolour very quickly!

A fleece blanket makes an excellent alternative to using towels. These feel luxuriously soft next to your client's skin. You can warm them on your radiator before placing them on your client, and they are quicker to dry than towels. Fewer towels more fleeces! If you don't have a radiator, you can warm them with hot water bottles or hot stones. If you work in a tropical country, you can just use pretty sarongs or silky material which are light and feel delicious on the skin.

Instead of using towels on feet, I used to use baby muslin cloths. Again, these are light, less bulky around the feet, and can be washed and dried very quickly.

Pillows

Small pillows are perfect for massage because they leave a space open by the shoulders and neck. You can buy a specially made pillow for this. Large pillows are more suitable for supporting you while working. For example, a large pillow placed between you and the couch will support your back and arms while doing ear candling, facials, or Indian head massage.

A V pillow with a small pillow placed in the small of the client's back will support the client during reflexology. It can also be used to support pregnant ladies on a seated massage chair. These are very comforting for young clients as they can snuggle into them, and they are incredibly supportive.

A wedge pillow under the legs is wonderful for reflexology, and a half-moon pillow under the knees is perfect for reducing pressure of the lower back during Reiki or massage.

I recommend that you use pillow protectors under clean, pressed pillowcases as oil can still seep through. You can use couch roll if you wish (see couch roll) to save on washing. For the half-moon cushion buy a UPU covered one.

A quick wipe with an antibacterial wipe is all that's needed to keep it clean.

Products

Always buy excellent quality products. The additional cost of these can be passed onto your clients. You cannot expect your clients to pay a premium for good quality therapy if you are using cheap oils or ear candles.

Music

If you play or record music in your therapy room or practice, you must use either royalty-free music or buy an annual music licence.

You can check whether you need to purchase a music license here. https://www.pplprs.co.uk

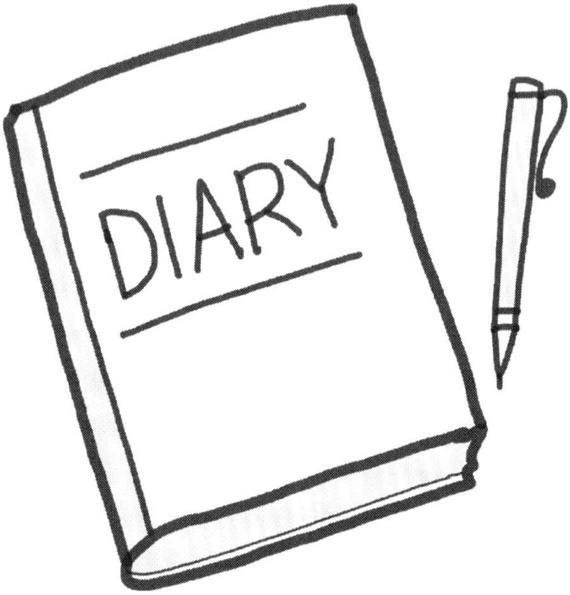
DIARY

APPOINTMENTS

Do not completely fill your diary with appointments. Always leave space for emergency clients. If you are contacted by a new client, it is best if you can see them quickly.

You are more likely to keep them as a client rather than they go somewhere else because they want to be seen sooner. That said, do not let clients make demands of your time. E.g., "I want to come today", or "I will only come at 3pm on Thursday". Appointment times should always be mutually agreed.

Dealing with "no-shows"

A no-show is not about a lack of respect for you. It is about the client not giving the time and effort to themselves. If you challenge them on their lack of commitment, they may get angry, but remember they are only mad at themselves. They may have a history of always putting themselves last.

Now that they have chosen to come for therapy, they must learn how, perhaps for the first time, to put themselves first. Equally, some clients may have been pushed around all their lives, and initially, may find it hard to adapt to a therapist giving them boundaries.

Notes and Ideas

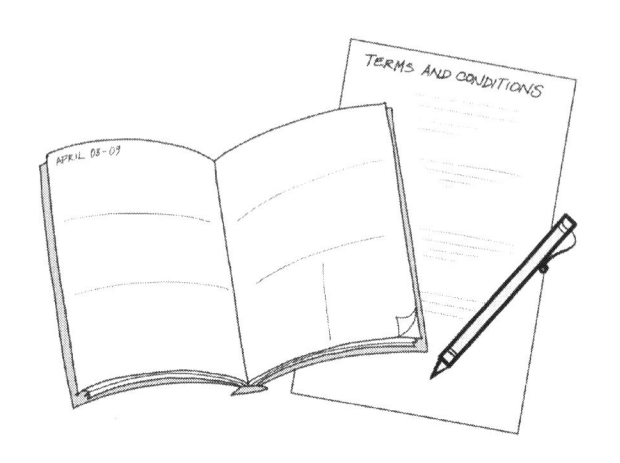

Terms and Conditions

Make it clear in your terms and conditions that the client is buying your time. You have given them an appointment and your time has been purchased.

I used to limp from month to month praying that my clients would return, and I would get paid. Now I take block bookings and ask for payment by bank transfer upfront. That way, a "no show" means I still get paid.

Write it in your terms and conditions that all charges or cancellations within 48 hours of the appointment are payable in full.

Obviously, if the client calls in the morning and says they have flu or have been sick all night, then you can choose to waive the fee. Still, I recommend that you always charge for forgotten appointments.

Manage client expectations

Many clients are looking for a quick, instant fix. Remind them this about them taking responsibility for their own wellbeing.

Sometimes, they just want to hand their problems over to you to fix, while they carry on as before. In cases like this, you'll need to explain that they will need to be an active partner in their own recovery.

- Sports therapists or chiropractors will often give clients physical exercises to do between sessions.

- Hypnotherapists will ask clients to listen to recordings or affirmations.

- Beauty therapists may expect their clients to follow a skincare regime.

If the client returns and says nothing has changed, then you must address what they are doing outside of your therapy room.

I often get asked "How many hypnotherapy sessions will I need? Sometimes, they question my recommended course of therapy and tell me that they are looking for a "quick fix".

When this happens, I tell them that you do not get a prescription from the doctors and expect to feel better after taking one pill. They understand this analogy.

Notes and Ideas

TIMEKEEPING

A client is buying a service from you but is also buying your time. If they are late for a good reason, e.g., there was an accident on the motorway then if you have time you can still give them the full hour or whatever your appointment time is.

If they were staying on at work to finish a job off when they knew they had a treatment booked, or they were out shopping (yes, I have had that excuse too) then I cut that time off their appointment.

I had one client who was once forty-five minutes late, and so I gave her fifteen minutes of Reiki.

This may sound harsh, but you need to teach your clients to value what you are providing. If they do not, they are not your ideal client.

Equally, you must stick to your appointment times. If you expect your clients to show up on time, then so must you.

CONFIDENTIALITY

During my hypnotherapy training, the tutor asked us to write down a deep secret on a piece of paper. We then folded it up and marked it with a symbol only we would recognise.

Initially, I was hesitant to do so, but, after some thought, I decided to embrace the exercise and complied.

We were then told to place them in a drawstring bag. The string was pulled, and the bag placed on the desk. The tutor said that she would come back to it later then continued with our lesson.

At the end of the lesson, I asked about the bag. Smiling, the tutor passed the bag around and asked us to reach in, find our piece of paper and take it out. Then she told us to take it home, rip it up or do whatever we liked with it.

I have never forgotten this powerful exercise. It showed how vulnerable you are when someone is holding onto your secrets.

Remember to thank your clients for their honesty, whenever they place their faith and trust in you. Sometimes they share things with you that they have never told anyone else. Respect their secrets.

KNOWING WHEN TO SHUT UP

Some clients love to talk and will explain every ailment that they have had since birth. In such cases, you will need to politely interrupt their "story" and ask them to focus only on what is relevant to their current issue.

They may have a friend that also comes to see you and will gossip about them. You can listen but do not pass on any information about them or comment.

If a client refers someone to you, they may be curious to know if that person made an appointment. To my mind, the most professional thing you can do is refuse to respond on the grounds of client confidentiality. However, this does very much depend on your type of business.

MALE THERAPISTS

I could not write this book without mentioning male therapists. There are many excellent male therapists. I feel some aspects of holistic therapy can be a tough profession for men. With men being the physically stronger sex, they can give excellent deep tissue massages and wonderful reflexology.

The problem is women! I don't understand how women can have a male hairdresser run their fingers through their hair but will not have an Indian head masseur. Or will throw their clothes off in front of male doctors but will not accept a relaxing aromatherapy massage from a male therapist.

I don't really know the answer to this one. All you can do is maintain your professionalism and perhaps combine your massage therapies with other complementary therapies.

BECOME AN EXPERT

When you become qualified, you want to help everyone. That's why you became a therapist, right?

If you are a beautician, you will have a long list of beauty treatments you can offer. The same goes for holistic therapy.

If you are continually adding services to your price list, your primary therapy becomes diluted.

Have you ever been to a restaurant that offers so many options on the menu that you find it impossible to choose?

My advice is simple - Think about what you love doing and then become an expert in it. When you do, you will become the "go-to" person for that therapy. For example, my hairdresser hates giving perms, so he stopped offering them. He has staff that do. A consultant I know only specialises in knee problems.

Think about combining your therapies into a package or programme. I used to specialise in fertility problems. I had problems myself, so I could relate to the heartache it can cause – (but you do not have to.) I combined reflexology and Reiki to help my clients get pregnant. Once they were pregnant, I changed this to Reiki only for the first trimester. Later, I offered a pregnancy massage. The third trimester was Hypnobirthing and pregnancy reflexology. After the baby was born Reiki and reflexology to balance the hormones.

You can see how I became the go-to therapist for fertility.

Once you know your niche, you will hone your skills. If you offer a long list of therapies, you cannot be expert at all of them, and so you risk being seen as a "master of none."

I always ask beauticians "What do you really love doing?" Some say nails, others say massage. When you love what you do, your clients will love you for the wonderful therapy you have given them. If you do not love what you do, they will know.

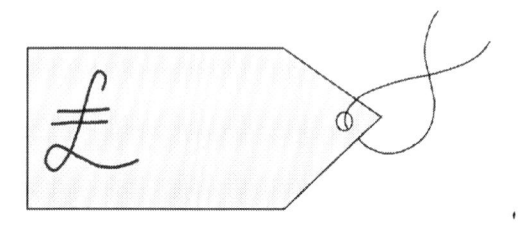

PRICING

There will always be someone that gives away their services or charges next to nothing. Equally, some therapists charge a fortune for what you do and are remarkably successful in doing so. Charge for what your services are worth and then some more. Do your research.

My aromatherapy tutor taught me to charge for the quality you are providing. If you are working in a small room that you are sharing with other therapists in a noisy location with no parking, then you must keep your prices low. If you are working from home and have a dedicated room or therapy summer house with private parking, you can charge more. If you are working in a plush private country club with a dedicated treatment room and private parking, you can charge even more.

I have never understood why mobile therapists charge less. Surely it makes sense that clients should pay more for the privilege (and convenience) of being seen in their own home? Plus, you will be adding mileage and travelling time to your fee.

It is the nature of owning your own business that your finances will fluctuate. During a time of recession put your prices up. Yes! Up! Think about it for a moment...

Inevitably you will have fewer clients because therapy is one of the first things clients let go of when money is tight.

You still have bills to pay, and like your clients, those bills will also have increased. Therefore, you'll have less money coming in and more money going out. So, the clients you do have will have to pay more to cover your expenses.

I like this quote "Good therapy isn't cheap, and cheap therapy isn't good".

Notes and Ideas

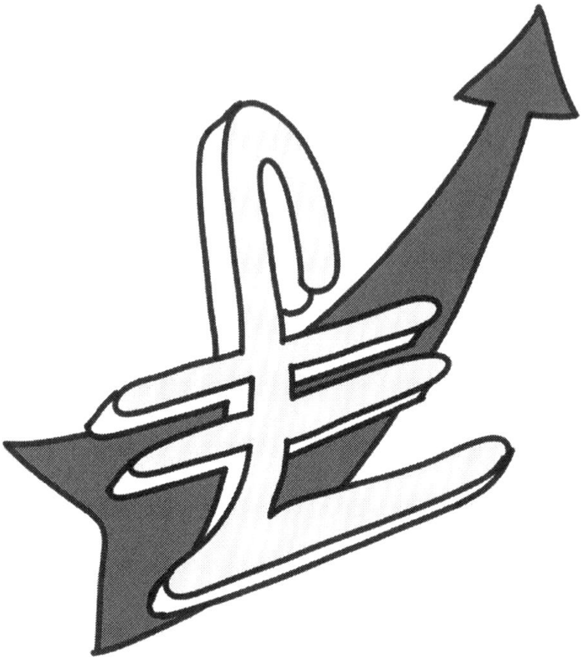

PRICE INCREASES

It is essential to make your client feel special, and they are not just coming along and paying you for a service.

When to increase prices?

I learnt the hard way that January is not a good time to increase your charges. Everyone is broke and are just getting over Christmas bills and the utility companies have all raised their prices. When I decide to increase my fees, I warn my clients in October that my charges will be going up in the new year. I will then explain that, because they are loyal customers, and to help them get over the festive period, I will not increase their fee until April.

Go ahead and increase your price for your new customers in January and to keep your existing clients happy increase their rates in April.

I recommend that you avoid falling into the trap of charging different client's different amounts. I have done that in the past and causes all sorts of problems. It's confusing for you as a therapist and also for whoever does your books and accounts. You even end up forgetting what you are charging each client.

DISCOUNTING

There are going to be genuine clients that want and desperately need help but who simply cannot afford your fees. They have done the rounds with various medical establishments and feel the only way forward is to pay privately for therapy.

I used to fall into the trap of offering discounts to elderly clients who were hesitating over my fee. This all comes down to a) being a carer in a caring profession, b) being soft, c) and most importantly having low self-esteem and not valuing your true worth.

Overcoming this expensive habit comes with experience. When you first set up your business, you may think yesterday, I was not qualified, today I am, and now I am let loose on the public. I can't justify charging what others charge.

Start by researching the local market. Find the cheapest and the most expensive and then set your price list somewhere in the middle. In the beginning, you may feel justified in charging less because you are recently qualified. If you do, remember to review your prices regularly and to increase them in line with your growing experience.

If a client caught a train or a bus to come and see you, you know they are committed. They have invested their time, money, and effort to see you.

I do not advertise my fees for this reason. It allows potential clients to contact me, have a free telephone consultation and then decide if it is for them **before** costs are even discussed. It really depends on what clients you want to help. You may not want to offer discounts at all and that is fine too.

If you are brave enough, try this line "If you are asking me to compromise my fee, what are you prepared to give up having this therapy improve your health?"

Another one is "When your car needs repairing or needs new tyres, do you pay for it?" They will say yes, then say "Well this is an investment in YOU and your health".

Be careful! Some clients will try it on. When I was struggling, newly qualified, holistic therapist, I gave a discount to a new client. Only to discover that she was off to the Bahamas on holiday the day after her first appointment! The same client asked me if I was going to give her a free treatment for Christmas. I told her politely "Actually, I think she should be giving me a Christmas bonus."

I used to wonder if these clients happily tip their waiter, hairdresser or taxi driver yet sometimes begrudge paying us, their therapist. This is why you must remember to point out the benefits to their health and wellbeing during every appointment!

Do we ask our dentist for a discount, or tell our doctor that the prescription is too expensive? Would you go into a supermarket, fill up your trolley and ask for a discount at the checkout?

Remind yourself of the many hours of expensive training and unpaid study, homework, and case studies that you did to get you where you are today.

Remind yourself of the ongoing expenses you must pay to be a professional therapist.

- The training, continuous professional development (CPD)
- Professional Insurance
- Professional Memberships
- Equipment and product costs
- Clinic rental and utility costs

You pay for what you get. How often when you are researching prices for something do you look at the cheap option and think that must be rubbish? You look at something expensive and think that must be worth it. You are worth it!

Charge accordingly.

I had a client complain once that her fee had increased during a recession. She said her gas and electric had gone up to which my reply was "So has mine!"

Notes and Ideas

LOYALTY SCHEMES

Loyalty schemes are popular. You could you have a loyalty card the size of a business card produced. This will have boxes that you could sign and date, and after so many appointments, when the card is full, you could offer a discounted therapy.

Sales tip:
Do not give away a full session. Offer an extra, like a mini facial or hand massage in addition to their full price therapy session.

REFERRALS

I have a referral scheme in place with some therapists. If I send them a client and that client become a regular, they pay me a referral fee.

If it fits with your business model, consider offering your clients a free session each time they refer a new client who books with you.

Only refer your clients to someone you have been to and are happy with. Think of your reputation.

Be a go-to person. I have business cards of other therapists that I can pass on to my clients. I regularly give out my chiropractor's business cards to my clients with back and joint pain. I no longer do reflexology, but I know someone that does. You cannot treat everyone, or you may not be offering what they require, but you can help them find someone you and they can trust.

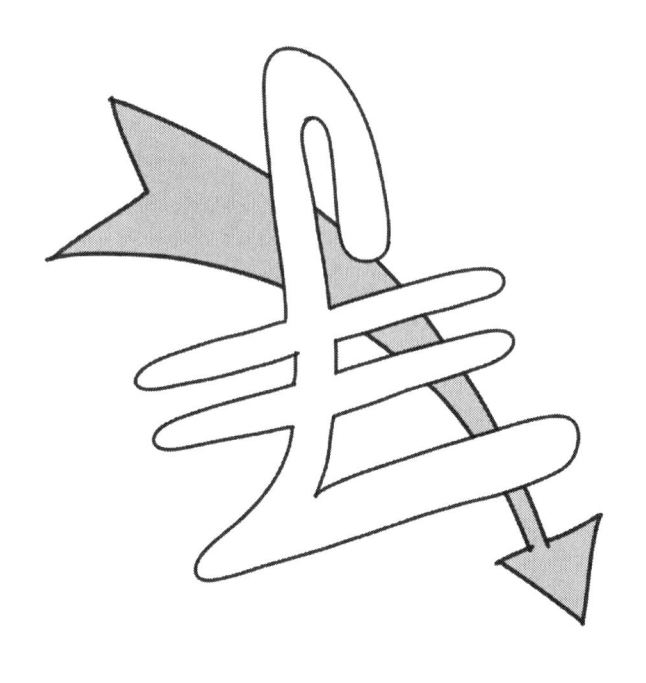

DISCOUNT VOUCHER SCHEMES

Do your homework. Research the options and ask others their opinion before embarking on a discount voucher scheme.

Discount voucher schemes can help to promote your business and are useful if you have just trained and want to get your name out there. But they can, if you are not careful, bust your budding business.

Limit how many you are going to sell. Once the limit has been reached, you will know how many bookings you need to fit in.

You will also be on a time limit, which means you will need to see all these clients by the deadline date, or you will not be paid by the voucher scheme!

Be careful with what you promote. Is it wise to discount your best-selling service to new customers and risk upsetting your regulars?

Wouldn't it make more sense to promote your cheapest service to get new customers through the door, so that you can then promote your more expensive therapies?

I know of one therapist who offered three beauty treatments on a discount voucher scheme and only earned £11 from each client (2014). When I called her to book a fully paid treatment, she replied that she could not fit me in as she had all her voucher scheme clients to fit in. Madness! Your priority are your regular clients, then new potentially regular clients, then vouchers. I did not return as she said she could not fit me, or her regular clients, in for a couple of months. Sadly, her business went bust.

Nothing is stopping you running your own discounted promotion and paying for local advertising and posting them on social media. You will make the rules, and you keep all your profit.

I learned that most voucher purchasers are not loyal customers. Most are voucher hoppers. You may get one or two that become regulars, but most of them will have already booked the next three therapies somewhere else by the time they see you.

Notes and Ideas

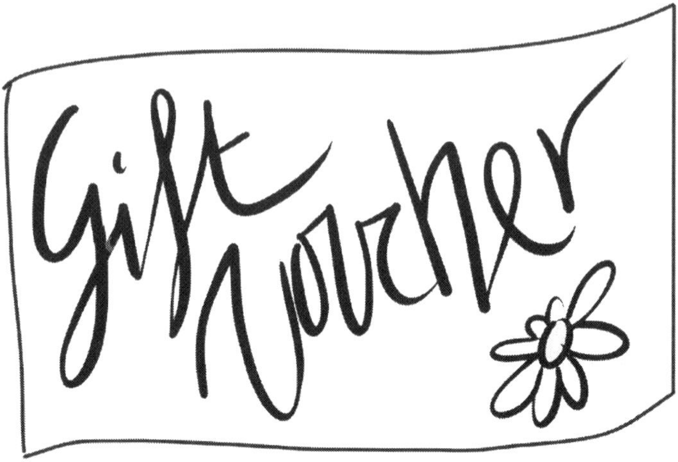
Gift Voucher

GIFT VOUCHERS

You can easily make up your own gift vouchers using Microsoft Word, Microsoft Publisher, or other graphic packages. You can then print them yourself or get them printed by an online or local printer. Keep a little book listing the following:

- Date sold
- Name of purchaser
- Name of recipient
- Therapy
- Price
- Expiry date

It is vital to put an expiry date on your voucher as you do not want someone calling you in three years for a therapy that you stopped doing two years ago.

Set a three, six, or twelve-month expiry date. Personally, I put three months on mine as I feel the less time you give them, the more likely they are to book in. Keeping a gift voucher logbook will serve to remind you of the details of the sale.

Most gift vouchers will not be used. If they are, most will not return. Do not take this personally.

Remember the voucher was purchased by someone who wanted them to come, not by the client. Make the voucher non-transferrable, so it is only to be used by the recipient.

Notes and Ideas

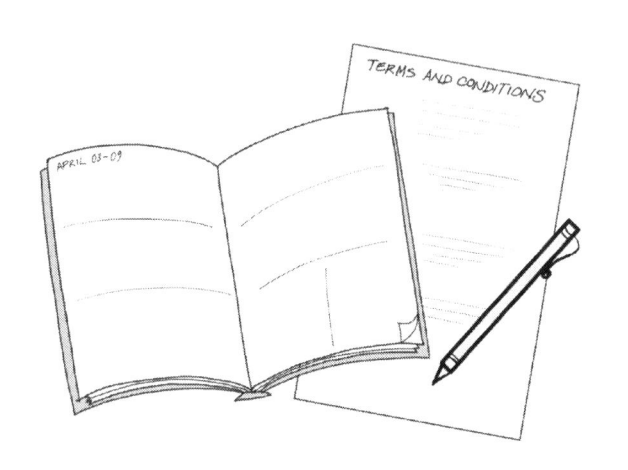

POLICIES, TERMS AND CONDITIONS

Put together your terms and conditions and send a copy to your client *before* they come for therapy. You are giving them details of what you expect of them and what they can expect of you. These will be specific to your business. For ideas on what to include, take a look at the policies at the bottom of my website

https://www.thespiritwithin.co.uk

QUALIFICATIONS

When you qualify in your chosen profession, you may get letters that you can you use after your name. These may be from your examining board or from a professional body that you belong to. Know what these letters mean. Most clients do not want to know, but some do. Be prepared when they ask you and tell them what you had to do to get them.

Use them on all your marketing. It gives you credibility. Your clients may check-up on them with your professional body.

INSURANCE

During your training, you will hopefully have been given some guidance on where to get your public liability insurance. Most will cover you for personal injury claims up to £10m. You can also get extra insurance for your room and your equipment.

When you are training, you may be able to get student insurance. Get insurance as soon as you start working with clients. Even if it's friends or family. You cannot assume that because they are friends or family, a claim will not be made, or they will not sue you if there is a problem.

You need to cover everything you are qualified to practice. I do not do any holistic therapy now. However, I am still fully insured just in case I do occasional reflexology or a massage for an old client, friend, or family member.

As you add more therapies to your price list, remember to add these to your insurance. I knew of one lady who was giving psychic readings as she was offering reflexology. The client got up and tripped over her couch lead and broke her ankle. The client sued, and when it went to the insurance company, the therapist got into a dispute because the client had said she was having reflexology and a reading. The therapist was insured for reflexology but not for giving readings!

Please be careful! If you are using essential oils, you must be a qualified aromatherapist. If you are using ear candles, you must be a qualified ear candler. **Use this simple rule, no qualification, no insurance. It's like driving a car, and you haven't passed your test.**

Clients will ask you; do you treat XYZ? If you are unsure about an illness, say so. It's better to say I need to check and then call your supervisor, do some research, ask your insurance company, or write to their GP before treating. **Remember, only practice what you are insured to practice.**

If you are looking for an insurance quotation here is a list to be getting started with:

https://www.fht.org.uk/insurance

https://www.hiscox.co.uk/business-insurance

https://www.swa.wildapricot.org//membership-benefits/insurance/

https://www.balens.co.uk

https://www.towergateinsurance.co.uk

Notes and Ideas

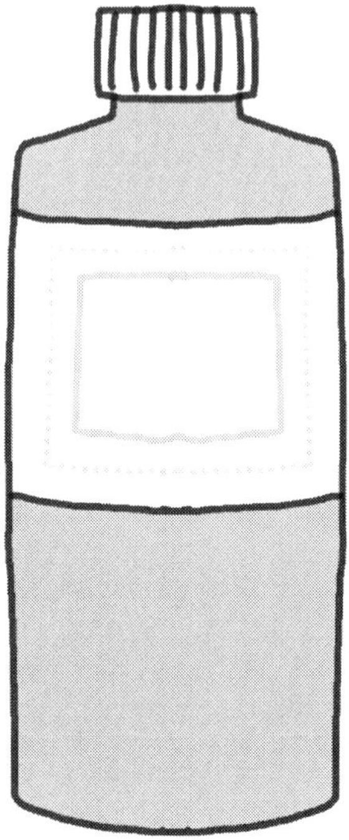

DRUGS

Get a copy of the BNF (British National Formulary) book from your doctor. This is the drug bible that doctors use in the United Kingdom. Your doctor will be able to give you an old copy as theirs is replaced twice a year. This is a handy reference tool to look up your client's medication to check for potential side effects.

This is particularly prudent if you are a hypnotherapist, as you cannot treat anyone who is on psychotic drugs. Please note, if you are not a qualified medical practitioner, you cannot give advice on the medicines your client is taking.

As your clients start to feel better about themselves if they are taking antidepressants, they may want to come off their drugs. Always insist that they do this only with their doctors' guidance. They must come off them slowly; otherwise, they can have severe reactions.

Refer your client back to their doctor if you feel that their drugs need checking. I had an extremely anxious lady. She was on thyroxine, and I asked her when she last had a review. She said she had not had one in six years. I recommended she got the dosage checked. Next time I saw her, the blood tests had proved that her medication needed changing, and she was feeling much better.

Notes and Ideas

PAY ATTENTION

Give your client 100% attention. If the telephone rings ignore it. Let the answerphone pick it up. Your client is paying you for a service and deserves your attention 100%. Be mindful of your contribution to their wellbeing and give them your complete attention.

TIME IS MONEY

I have two clocks in my therapy room. One is by the side of my client's head (ensure this clock does not have an audible tick) The second is hanging on the wall in front of me, but behind my client. As humans, we rarely stare into someone's eyes all the time we are talking. When your client briefly looks down or away, you can quickly glance at the clock to check on the time without breaking your concentration on your client.

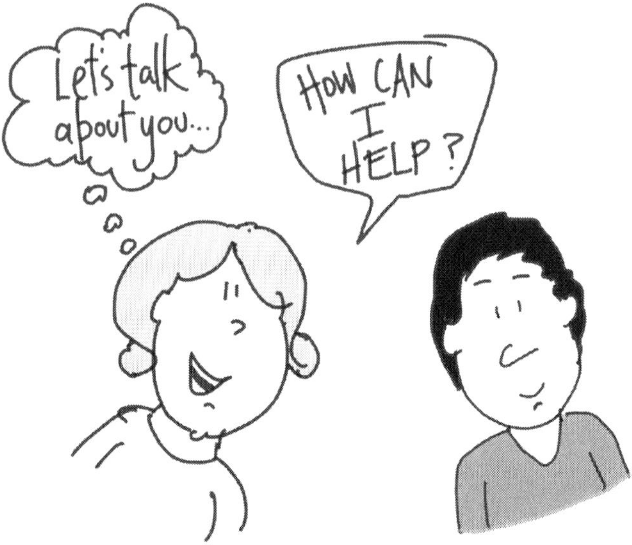
Let's talk about you...
HOW CAN I HELP?

CLIENTS TELLING YOU WHAT TO DO

When you have clients that love to be in control, they feel out of their comfort zone and will want to advise you.

I have been told my lampshade is not straight, my curtains have not been taken up correctly, that I should have tinted windows as the sun shines too brightly in my room. I have even been told that I had cobwebs in my outside porch!

It is how you handle them that matters, and I usually do that with humour and lots of "Oh dear, never mind," and then distract them by asking them a question.

You may have a caring, nurturing client who wants to ask about you and if you make sure that you look after yourself. This can sometimes be a distraction because they do not want to talk about themselves.

They may want to know about your home and your family life. It is essential to recognize this for what it is and steer the conversation back to them. After all, they are paying you for a service, not a chat with a friend. Stay professional and business-like while being friendly.

Notes and Ideas

I AM SO BUSY!

We all have highs and lows in self-employment. However, when a client calls do not let them know you have been sitting by the telephone waiting for it to ring. It is far better to make time for their appointment seem limited rather than saying that you can see them anytime. If you say you have plenty of availability, they will question whether they have contacted the right therapist.

A smart trick is to flick through your diary (even if it is empty) or tap on your computer keyboard, make some Mmm noises and say "Ah, I can see you at 2pm on Tuesday, is that any good?!" This gives them the impression that you are busy and that they are lucky to get an appointment with you.

I MUST GO

When a client calls you for the first time, they naturally want to check you out. They want to have a chat to make sure you are the right person to help them. This initial conversation also allows you to assess them before deciding whether you want to take them on as a client. This is called a <u>free telephone consultation</u> and should not be confused with free therapy.

It is acceptable for them to call back again once they have discussed with a family member, but remember, you are not there to listen to all their problems on the telephone. As they say in sales, you need to close the deal. If you find it hard to end the conversation without sounding rude, here is another trick for you…

If you are working from home, open your front door and ring your own doorbell and say "Sorry, I must go…I have a (paying) client that's just arrived".

COLDS AND FLU

If a client cancels their appointment due to a cold or flu, recommend they drink plenty of fluids. They could use fresh lemon and ginger in warm water to help with a liver cleanse and ease their throat. Tell them to hug themselves when coughing. This will help with that awful bruised feeling in their chest if they have a hacking cough.

I have it written in my terms of service that I do not want clients attending their appointment if they are suffering from a cold or believe they are starting a cold.

I have turned clients away at the door who are full of cold. I do not want it, and I do not wish to the germs left in my therapy room for my next client.

RENTING A ROOM

I can only really talk about my own experience. I have written this book as if you are working from home, as I do.

I worked in a chiropractor's clinic. I wanted to do relaxing holistic work, but all they wanted me to do was deep tissue massage on their clients. Their hygiene was so bad that I was embarrassed to work there, so I left.

I rented a room from two masseuses', and I got zero work as they took every new enquiry for themselves.

I was about to rent a room for hypnotherapy at different chiropractor's practice, and she just wanted me to do discounts so that she could gain new clients.

I also had an experience at a doctor's surgery (see Working with the NHS).

These are my only experiences, and I was made to feel like I was not self-employed at all. The people I rented from wanted to tell me what to as if I was a member of the staff even though I was the one paying them!

I am not saying it does not work. I know of many therapists who would never work from home and have fantastic rooms they rent.

You will have to shop around and find a location that suits you. It doesn't have to necessarily fit in with what you are offering, but it will certainly help. Trying to hypnotise someone in the back of a noisy hairdressing salon will not work!

When looking for room rental look at the location. Do you have a receptionist who is invested in your business? Are you working with other therapists that compliment what you do, or are they direct competition?

Do your research before investing. Ask other therapists for information and price comparisons.

Does the room suit you? Will you have to share with others?

One of my colleagues hired a room that belonged to a physiotherapist. Every time he turned up, he had to move out lots of gym balls and other equipment and then return them all to the room afterwards. This will add to your setting up and clearing time.

Is the room cleaned by you, or do you pay for a cleaner? If you are sharing the room, does the other occupant share the same cleanliness standards?

Is there convenient parking and easy access for your clients?

Do they book directly with you, or do you have a receptionist?

Who takes the money? What are their fees?

The list goes on, but I hope this has given you some solid ideas to think about.

WORKING IN A SALON

I have never worked in a salon, spa, or therapy practice. The whole idea of me being self-employed was to work for myself.

I can only comment on what I have been told by the several therapists I know who have worked in spas.

Working in a spa can provide you with:

- Comradeship/friendship
- Lunch
- Training
- Experience
- Uniforms
- Laundry
- Products
- Room
- Utilities
- Towels
- Regular income

- Clients
- Support
- Spa access
- Discounts
- Safety
- Security

The downside is you will be working to their schedules. I had a nineteen-year-old who came to me after working in a spa for two years. She had a damaged spine and extremely painful hands.

I discovered their receptionist was booking back-to-back massage appointments with no break for her in between. She was a brilliant therapist but gave it up for the sake of her own health.

Another therapist worked in a spa and again was working doing back-to-back massages. She fell pregnant and was fired. Yes, it still does happen.

You will see what the spa is charging the clients and may compare it to what you are getting paid, and this may create some resentment. This is not an ideal state of mind to be in for you or your clients. Working in a spa or salon does give you a safety net. You may like the interactions with staff members, or you may wish to gain valuable experience and then drop the safety net and go solo. Feel the fear and do it anyway. It may be scary at first, but it really does give you the freedom to do what you want.

Notes and Ideas

VOLUNTEERING

Charities will always try and get as many donations as they can. We all like to give, which is why we do what we do. Stop and review how much time and effort you want to give to charity. One day per month for free is acceptable and is still helping a charity out.

A lot of complementary therapists volunteer their services. This is where there is confusion over two words that sound the same but are spelt differently. Complementary = complementary therapy is complementary to allopathic medicine. E.g., complementary to GP or hospital treatments. It used to be called alternative therapy, or new age therapy and sometimes it still is.

Complimentary = giving your services away for free.

You must ask yourself; can I afford a day off while working unpaid? If you can, then do it and enjoy it. But do make sure you get something back in return.

Have your powders and creams supplied for you or get your travel expenses covered. There must be an exchange for what you do. Otherwise, it is undermining the value of your services, your clients will not appreciate it, and you will start to resent doing it.

Free appointments mean the client has not committed to part with any money, so it does not matter to them if they postpone, cancel or worse still not show up.

Make it worth your while. Set your boundaries with the place you are working in. For example, state that you will only come in for a minimum of six bookings and will take no more than nine in a day. This depends, of course, on the type of therapy you are offering.

See if you can charge even a nominal amount. Some organizations and charities will pay their therapists.

Just because other therapists give their services away for free, it does not mean you have to feel guilty and do the same. Set the bar and others may follow suit. Put free therapies through your expenses stating your usual fee and making your petty cash slip as pro bono. Also, remember to claim for your travelling and parking charges.

NOTES AND IDEAS

WORKING FROM HOME

You need to be disciplined to work for yourself at home. During "working" hours, I am always working. I am either seeing clients in my therapy room, or I am in my office, doing administration, online networking or working on my website.

One of my colleagues sits in front of her television with her laptop on her lap. This does not work for me and does not sound very productive.

It is easy to get drawn into social media or shopping websites. I have an egg timer on my desk. If I am having an administration day, I set it for every half an hour. I have half an hour working on my computer and half an hour putting the washing on, changing the bed and other chores. I do this throughout the day. It helps me gets my tasks done, and it stops me becoming tired working on the computer all day.

I have a lot of therapists that say working from home is lonely. If you have a good business and are running it well, you cannot be alone. Make friends with other therapists.

When your business is quiet, theirs will be too. Meet up, work on a project together, have coffee or lunch. It will really help you stay connected and happy.

Notes and Ideas

WORKING ONLINE

There are a variety of apps that you can use for online consultations with your clients or online networking meetings. You can use Zoom, Skype, or WhatsApp for your talk therapies. Here are a few things to think about while working online.

When doing talk therapy with a client you must ensure that they are safe and are not going to be disturbed. I recently called a client and he was still in work; this is not suitable for talk therapy. During the consultation ask for an emergency contact name and number. If doing hypnotherapy state before, and at the start of hypnosis if they do not hear your voice for fifteen minutes they will naturally wake up. This way if you lose connection for any reason they will not have to worry.

Make sure you have good lighting behind your laptop or device so that your face is well lit. I see many people working in poor light, in a dim room or with a window or bright light behind them. This kind of setup means that your face will be silhouetted and the other people on the call won't be able to see you clearly. I see it all the time and believe me, it doesn't look very professional.

Try placing your laptop in front of a window for good natural light but be careful that you are not being blinded by sunlight which will make your face look washed out. Alternatively, buy a USB lighting ring which you can place behind your laptop, to illuminate your face. This will give you a pleasantly soft, diffused light.

Think about your background. A plain wall or a bookcase makes an excellent background. Remember, your clients will notice what is behind you. They don't want to see the children's toys, your ironing, or your kitchen work surfaces! Some of the apps allow the use of a green screen which means you can use different virtual backgrounds. In addition to the built-in images, you can create your own, branded virtual backdrop using Microsoft Word or PowerPoint. You can include your message, tagline, and logo, save it as a Jpeg and then upload it to your chosen software. It will look much more professional than the Starship Enterprise or Yoda. Be sure to test your virtual background to ensure it works well, and don't wear anything green! It can be very distracting if parts of you become invisible. If you cannot use a virtual background, position one or two pop up banners behind you if you have them.

Use a good camera that gives a bright, clear image. Up to date laptops or mobile phones have excellent cameras, older machines do not! Make sure you clean the camera lens from time to time.

Use the mute button if you are coughing or sneezing or the phone suddenly rings.
Switch off your video AND your sound if you need to use the bathroom. I know of one colleague who needed the toilet urgently. He ran off forgetting to switch off the audio and returned to a "room" of laughing people who had heard everything.

Even if you are working online from home, remember to take care of your appearance. Wear makeup do your hair and wear a suitable smart top. If you are sitting in your shorts or pyjama bottoms, remember if you have to stand up for any reason, they will see this.

Put your laptop, landline and mobile on do not disturb and ask your clients to do the same.

While you may find pets walking across your desk amusing and your children waving cute, your clients may not. Put up a do not disturb sign outside your door to make sure that you can dedicate your time and focus 100% of your attention on your client.

If you are attending an online networking event, remember to prepare and practice your 60-second pitch, or presentation online with a friend, so that you can get some constructive feedback before going live.

Being online makes it harder to make a positive first impression as clients cannot read your body language so well.

Pace yourself on your use of online work. There is a thing called Zoom fatigue, where you can feel quite exhausted after a day online. There are a three of reasons for this phenomenon.

Firstly, when you are in a meeting staring at the screen, it looks as if everyone is focused on you.

Secondly, others in the meeting are usually on mute, and that can make you feel quite nervous too.

Finally, just sitting indoors, staring at a computer for long periods can make you feel tired anyway.

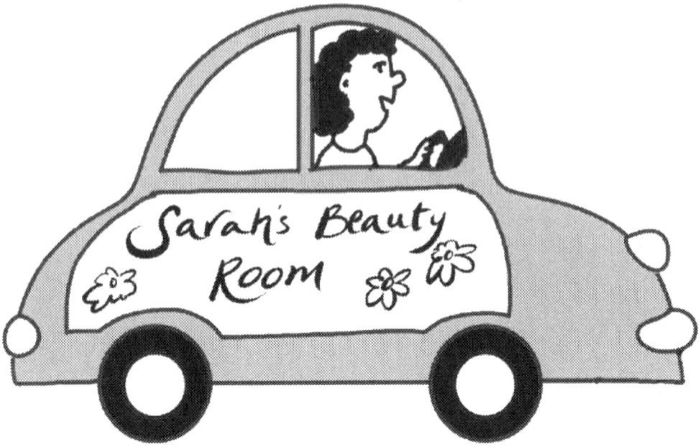
Sarah's Beauty
Room

MOBILE THERAPY

Apart from fairs, I have only done mobile work a few times. The first was Reiki in someone's flat, and I found that I didn't have enough space to work around the client. Another was doing ear candles for a family. When I put my couch back in my car after work, I strained my back.

Think about the equipment you will have to carry. And remember, nobody is going to help you load and unload your car every hour of your working day.

WORKING WITH THE NATIONAL HEALTH SERVICE (NHS)

I have books that are 30 years old, and they say that times are changing, and complementary therapy will be big in the NHS soon. Unfortunately, we are still waiting.

I know of some therapists that work in an NHS surgery and get plenty of referrals, but examples like this are few and far between.

I recently approached one of my local surgeries with a view to working with them. I was told I could pay for a shared surgery room but could only work on a Saturday morning behind a closed door. I would not be allowed to advertise in the surgery or even put my leaflets in the waiting room, and I would receive no recommendations from staff or doctors. You can imagine my response!

WORKING WITH FAMILIES

Working with families is extremely rewarding. You can see the family dynamics from different viewpoints. Always ensure you treat each client individually and under no circumstances, repeat what the other family members have said.

If you see clients out and about, shopping with their families, either avoid them or, if they have seen you, say hello and carry on walking. Remember, clients may not have disclosed to their partners; they are coming to see you. If you just said hello, they could say you are just someone from their workplace. I am saying this from a talk therapist's point of view

WORKING WITH CHILDREN

If you choose to work with children, have suitable items available for them. A small chair, a children's blanket and a small pillow with a children's pillowcase will make them feel more comfortable and nurtured.

I have a V pillow with changeable cases, which they can wrap around themselves to really feel safe. You could have a small selection of toys or books. Children often bring their own favourite toy, and this should be encouraged.

Depending on their age children may like to pick a pebble, shell, or crystal from a bowl I keep. I tell them to take with them, and that it can be their courage talisman.

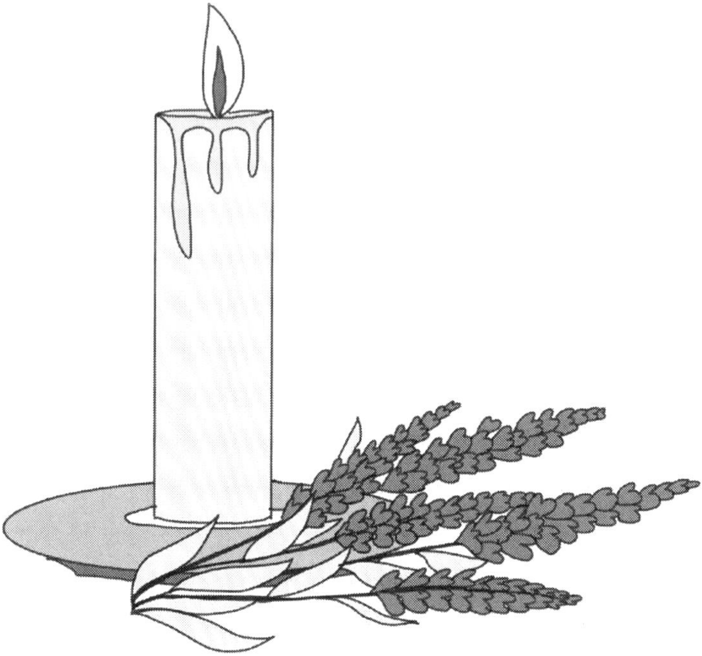

ABREACTIONS

As a therapist, you must always be prepared in case a client has an abreaction. This is a release of a previously repressed emotion, achieved through reliving the experience that caused it.

This can happen during talk therapy but also in any kind of healing or hands-on treatment. If a client lives alone and has not had someone's tender touch for a long time, they may burst into tears after a massage.

Allow them to cry. This is a healing reaction and one that is beneficial to the client as it a release of pent up emotion. When we are stressed, our body is flooded with cortisol. By having a good cry, cortisol is released from our system, leaving us feeling better than before.

Offer your clients some tissues after they have cried, not during. Offering tissues implies that you want them to stop to make you feel better. Offer them a drink of water afterwards, and do not hug them. You are their therapist, not their friend.

Always ensure that your client leaves in a positive state. Ask them what they are doing afterwards, and what positive things they have planned. This will help them focus on something else.

You may feel very moved by a client's reaction and find it hard sometimes to hold back your own tears. It is OK to not be OK, and sometimes clients will warm to you for having done so.

When you first start your business, you may find that you feel very emotional about your client's needs. As you gain experience, you will learn how to put boundaries in place and not be affected by their abreaction. This does not make you hard. You can still be empathic, but you are not reacting to their problems or issues.

Some clients may want to hug you when they leave. Respond appropriately to your clients' needs, but you should not be the one offering the hug as it may make them feel uncomfortable.

Sometimes, as we work with clients, they may become angry. As we start to release the tension they are holding in their body or mind, we may be stirring up buried emotions. The client may become angry towards you and what you are doing to them. Explain this is perfectly natural and expected. Do not take this anger personally. It is not directed at you.

Clients may even leave and not come back. They may not yet be ready to confront the emotions. Do not take this as a rejection. They may need time to process things and come back to you later.

CONTACT INFORMATION

When I started my business, I gave out my mobile number. I quickly got fed up with clients texting me to move their appointments, cancel their appointments, or even phone for a chat (free counselling) at inappropriate times. I put a stop to this when a client called me at 9.30pm one Saturday night. I quickly changed my contact details to my landline, complete with an answerphone. Clients would not call their dentist, doctor, or hairdresser on the weekend, so why should they do it to their therapist?

As the use of the internet continues to expand, I find that more clients now email. It also opens the possibility of offering online appointment booking and even online consultations.

This way, you can set the boundaries. If a client calls or emails at the weekend, I return the call or email on Monday morning.

One of my colleagues has a separate mobile for her business. This seems too much like hard work for me and somewhat dated. (I am thinking here of my time in the corporate world when I had a personal mobile and a work one).

It really depends on what works for you. The way I look at it is, when the practice is shut, it is shut. An alternative is to pay for separate numbers, one is for private callers, and the other is for business. You can then quickly identify each type of call on your mobile and see who is calling you. Then you can decide whether you wish to accept the call or not.

Set your boundaries. If a client calls me at 8pm on a Friday night, I return the call on Monday morning. Set the ground rules from the beginning.

You may occasionally lose clients this way because they feel they need an instant response. But if they expect you to be on call for them 24/7, you are better off without them, as they will always demand that level of response from you.

If you are a talk therapist, you may have people threaten self-harming or suicide. In this case refer them to their doctor, the Samaritans, or other groups in your area. You are not responsible for them outside of your business hours.

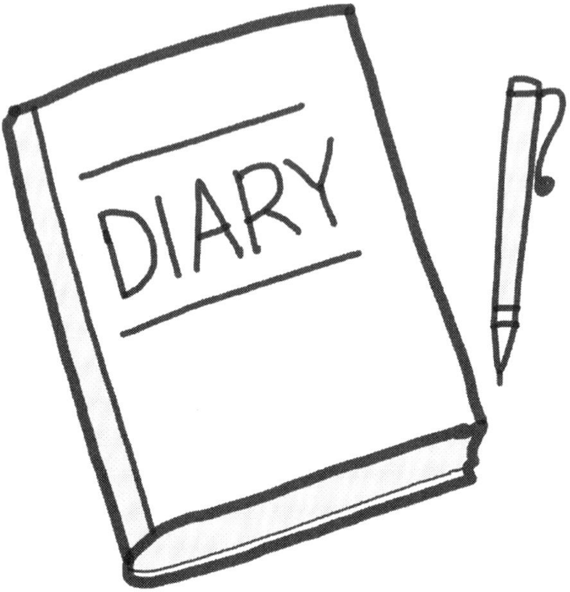
DIARY

DIARY MANAGEMENT

Most of my clients these days use the calendar on their mobile phone. Personally, I prefer a paper diary. I always write in ink and put add the annotation (P/P) if they postpone or (Canx) if they cancel. On the initial consultation, I put in their name, telephone number and the code (I/C) plus what they are coming for and the price.

Once they have paid, I write either (C) for cash payment, (CH) for a cheque or (BACS) for bank transfer and the date of transfer. This, of course, is my personal system and you are welcome to copy or adapt it. Alternatively, find a system that works better for you.

Using a paper diary, you do not have to worry about on-line data being stolen, your computer crashing or your mobile phone battery dying. I leave my diary at home, locked in my therapy room, so I know it is safe. It will not be hacked or left on a train somewhere.

At the end of the week, I do my accounts. I mark with a P in red pen, (paid) and an S in green pen (spreadsheet). This means the fee has been paid into the bank and I have added it to my account's spreadsheet. At the end of the year, my diary is burnt.

There are a plenty of software applications available that allow you to offer appointment booking online. Your clients can book their appointment via their computer or phone, and you can send text and email reminders.

Some of these are free. Remember, you are using third-party software. Can you trust the supplier, and are they reliable? What happens if they suddenly stop trading? You will also need to register under the data protection act. You can find out about this here.

https://www.gov.uk/data-protection

THIRD-PARTY SOFTWARE

We are used to using technology for so many things: emails, apps for bookings and banking. I use Dropbox for my clients' invoices, receipts, my terms of service policy and hypnotherapy recordings. You must notify your clients that you are using third party software if it involves them and what you are using it for. Put this in your terms of service policy.

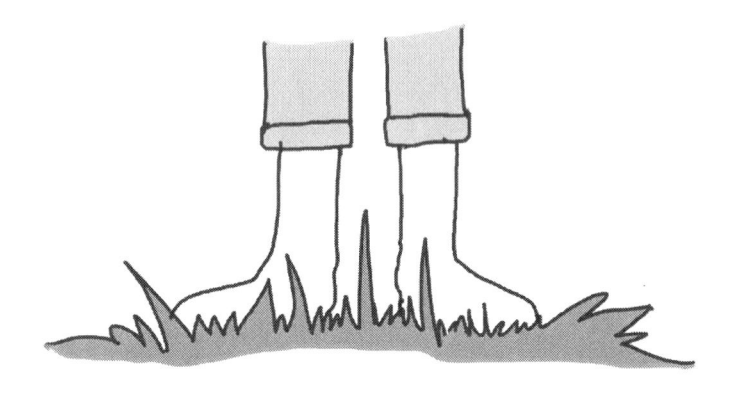

AFTERCARE

You will know from your training what aftercare advice to give to your clients. It's always good practice to allow five minutes before your client leaves to provide them with a glass of water and make sure they are grounded.

You can use biodegradable cups which are not only hygienic, but it also saves on you washing loads of glasses at the end of the day.

If they are still feeling woozy get them to stand up and stamp their feet. This will help centre them and get them feeling like they are back in their body.

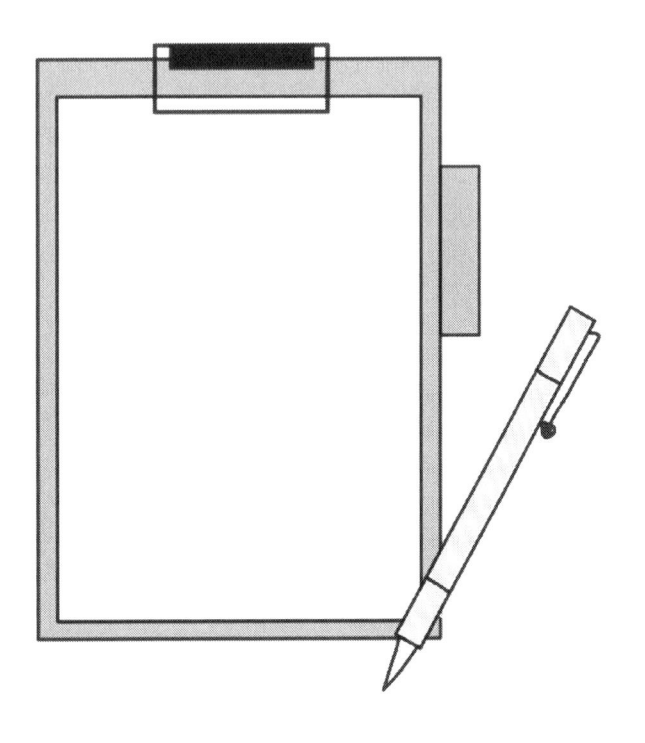

NOTE TAKING

You should have been trained in taking notes during your training because good records can help you provide a high standard of care.

You may think that you have a good memory but, at the end of a long day seeing many clients, you will inevitably forget some of what you did. Either take notes as you go or write out a post-it note for each session and then write up your notes at the end of the day.

Your notes need to be securely stored in a fireproof lockable cabinet or drawer accessible only by you.

Some therapists like to write copious notes. Others write little. If you are typing them up on a computer, they must be encrypted. You can do this by purchasing encryption software or use just your client's initials, or a number so only you can identify them. Look up the data protection act here.

https://www.gov.uk/data-protection

I do not save clients emails. If you want to keep them, print them off and put them in their files.

Be careful with your notes, always keep them professional and factual. Your clients have a right to read their notes. They must formally ask for these in writing and it is up to you how much you wish to disclose to them.

Full and clear client records are essential for your therapy insurance policy to have the best chances in defending any allegations of negligence or injury.

They could be requested in a court of law, so be mindful about what you are writing.

The General Data Protection Regulation (GDPR) provides the following rights for individuals:

- The right to be informed
- The right of access
- The right to rectification
- The right to erasure
- The right to restrict processing
- The right to data portability
- The right to object
- Rights concerning automated decision making and profiling

This and more information can be found at https://www.ico.org.uk

NOTES AND IDEAS

GIFTS FROM CLIENTS

When I worked in the corporate world, I found that different companies had different policies. In one, if I was given a client gift, I was able to keep it. In another, I was told I was not to accept gifts. In a third, all contributions were pooled together and shared with my colleagues. Now you are self-employed you make your own rules.

It is always lovely to receive a bouquet or a gift from a grateful, appreciative client. It is also fantastic for posting on social media. It makes them, and you feel great, so why refuse it?

Occasionally, I will give a client a gift. If they have had a bereavement or are having a particularly tough time, then a gift of a book, flowers or even a card can make someone feel even more cared for.

It shows them that they are more than just a client. You can put the gifts through your expenses claim.

I would, however, draw the line at having a coffee or lunch with a client. I had one client who I was treating for infertility. When she got pregnant, she was so grateful that she called me up and asked me to go for a coffee and cake with her. I declined, saying that I was too busy, but that I was extremely pleased with her news. Remember, they are your clients – not your friends.

COMPLAINTS

Just as in any job, you can occasionally have a client complain. When this happens, it is essential to remain calm and in control and remember that this is not a personal attack on you. Listen, listen, and listen again.

Early on in my therapy career, I had a client email me a complaint saying that I was giving her a sales pitch about all the therapies I offered.

I was used to doing this in my previous life in the corporate world. I took this as valuable feedback, and it led to a change in my consultation practice.

- Take a complaint on board
- What could you have done differently?
- What can you change to improve?
- Was the complaint justified?

Often, we can be dealing with angry clients. They have come to you for help, and sometimes they feel worse before they start to feel better. (See Abreaction). Set this up in their first appointment by saying "Sometimes you will leave here feeling fantastic, other times you may wonder what she has done to me? This is all part of the healing process".

If a client contacts you by email and asks for a refund, call them for a discussion. Explain that you can't give them a refund as they have bought your time and that a service has been provided.

If you offer a refund or another session you are admitting the session was substandard, so do not do it. The customer is always right, but remember you are the boss, and sometimes you must assert your authority.

You cannot make all your clients love you – let them go – do not be needy. You are the therapist, right? - move on.

MARKETING

Business Cards and Leaflets

Be consistent with all your marketing material. Make sure your business cards, leaflets and website use the same logo and colours.

It is worth creating your own logo and having a graphic designer produce it for you. You can then use this anywhere. It will be unique to you and your business. Some people may copy your design, but it will never be exactly the same.

When you are starting out, you can use online marketing to produce your business cards and leaflets. When you can afford it, invest in getting them firstly created by a professional graphic designer and then produced by a local printer.

I would recommend matt laminate finish with a high graded paper on your business cards. They have a great feel to them, and the colours look crisp. You can also use soft touch, but these can be difficult to write on. I use several different cards. Matt laminate appointment cards are easy to write on, soft touch business cards to display or give out at networking meetings. I also use specialist cards for the armed forces in the force's colours. It is still my logo but ties in with their colours.

Always have your business cards on you. Keep some in your car so if you are out and about without your purse or wallet you will still have some to give out, should the opportunity arise.

Put your cards anywhere and everywhere. Speak to everyone your meet about your business and if appropriate, give them a card. Ask in shops if they have a restroom where they can put your cards on their notice board.

I have gotten business from chip shops, garden, and community centres, cafes, restrooms, convenience stores and even doctors' surgeries.

Company name or personal name?

While it is good practice to be consistent with your company name and logo, it makes sense to be consistent with your own name too.

If you are giving out a business card with your name on it, it should be the name you are known by. I am known by Deborah, and that is my name across all social platforms and any form of marketing. There is no point in being Debbie on one site and Debs on another.

I was recently given a business card, and it said the company name but just "Jack" as the person's name. I found it difficult to connect with Jack as I didn't know his surname. Make it easy for your clients and colleagues to connect with you.

I know quite a few therapists who have dropped their company name and only use their personal name. This is a personal choice. Again, be consistent. Know who you are.

Uniform

If you wear a uniform, consider having your logo and company name printed on the front and the back. I used to have a polo shirt with my company name embroidered on the left breast. I also had a couple embroidered in more prominent writing across the back. These are great when you are walking about or working at fairs.

Name badges

It is easy to make your own name badge for networking events. The more events, workshops, and courses you go on the more lanyards and name badges you will acquire. You can easily slip your own badge design into them.

Pens/giveaways

Personally, I prefer pens. Pens are useful. And, unlike your business card, they can be left anywhere. People like pens. People like free stuff but for maximum impact and retention make your giveaway useful and exciting.

Some people use food, for example, chocolates or jellybeans. I would recommend being careful about this.

- What if your client is overweight and they are coming to you for weight loss?

- What if your client is diabetic?

- What if the parent has taught their child to never accept sweets from a stranger?

- What if the parents are controlling their child's E numbers?

You won't have any of these problems with a pen.

Bookmarks are also useful and make a great form of advertising, especially if you have a lovely design on one side and your company details on the other.

One holistic therapist I know had bookmarks and fridge magnets made by an online company and was selling them at a fair! Now you may be thinking "Why would anyone buy something that advertises you on it?" OK, I know stately homes and museums do it all the time. Still, they are selling a much higher volume and better-quality products, and the idea of it is that it is a souvenir. You will be lucky if you find a client who keeps a memento of their time spent with you.

Branded Angel cards (*see Giveaways*)

These are great as I find that most of my clients love them. On one side is just one word or several words of encouragement. On the other side is my company name, website and telephone number. It gives them hope and inspiration, so they keep them. One client keeps them on a noticeboard at home, another pasted them in a scrapbook, a third carries them with her in a tin in her handbag. Every time they look at them, they will be reminded of their time and experience with you.

BRANDING

Be your own brand. One Sunday afternoon, I sat down with a blank piece of paper and wrote down what I wanted for the following:

- Company name
- Logo
- Tagline
- Colour scheme
- What my company stands for (mission statement)

Come up with your own ideas, and then you can look at others. Do not copy others' ideas and refrain from plagiarism on your website. It's not cool, it's not professional, and it's not yours. When you use your words from your heart, then they will be authentic, and this will shine through.

ADVERTISING

Work out what your company stands for. What are your ethics? What is your aim?

Here is a simple exercise to help you put together your advertisement. You can also use this in your marketing.

Why?

Why do clients need you? What can you offer to help them?

We will work together to...

How will you work together? What will you help them achieve?

The solution

What can they expect from your therapy? How will it make them feel?

Who?

Who is your ideal client? What sort of client are you looking for?

NOTES AND IDEAS

WHERE TO ADVERTISE

Website

When I started my business in 2000, a friend created my website. I was number one on Google for five years, mainly because nobody else had a website at the time. Nowadays, I believe it is essential that anyone running any kind of business has a website.

Google and social media

Look into Google and social media advertising. These do work. I will not say too much about them here as the rules change consistently.

Local magazines

The local magazines are an effective way for therapists to advertise. These A5 glossy magazines that are local to a particular postcode area. It is good to work out a deal with the publishers allowing you to promote yourself in two areas on alternative weeks.

Leaflet drop

Try it. Some work, some do not. As long as what you are producing is not costing you a lot of time, money and effort. Will you do the drop, or will you pay someone to do it for you? Are you printing them yourself, or are you getting a graphic designer to design and print for you?

Business cards

Put them anywhere and everywhere. It is a cheap way of advertising. Put them on any notice board you can find.

- Newsagents
- Chip shop
- Cafés
- Restaurant
- Local supermarket
- Chemist
- Doctors
- Hospitals
- Dentists
- Mind body spirit shops
- Clubs
- Pubs

- Health shops
- Spas
- Therapy Centres
- Mind body spirit fairs
- Community centres

Give them to friends and family so that they can pass them on. Give them to your existing clients to do the same.

Hospitals and Doctors Surgeries

Don't be ripped off by telephone calls from companies offering advertising in hospitals or doctors' surgeries. People that work there and go there believe in orthodox therapy, so why would they be interested in reading about complementary therapies?

A colleague of mine spent thousands on advertising on a hospital map. The map had pockets that would hold his cards. He paid his money which tied him into a two-year contract. When he visited the hospital, he found the map hidden behind a door by the lifts with no cards on display. He went back to the company to cancel the second year but found he couldn't as he had signed a contract and agreed to their terms and conditions.

Hospital Radio

If someone is listening to it, the chances are they have already had surgery and are not feeling up to doing much. The same goes for hospital magazines. You could argue that if the client is not getting the answers through conventional therapy, they may read about your alternative. I believe you would be wasting your money. They can look up the alternatives and do their research on the internet.

Newspaper

Local papers are always crying out for local news, so why not write articles or news releases and send them in? Because an article is not an advert, people are much more likely to read it. It should be topical. It could be about you celebrating 20 years as a local business or launching a new product or service for your local community. Such articles raise your profile by piquing interest in your business.

Local radio

A lot of people listen to local radio, and so it is an ideal place to showcase you and your business.

You can have an interview broadcast with one of the presenters, often for free. You can also advertise on there. It can be quite costly but check first in case your assumptions are wrong.

Podcasts

I cannot really comment on these as I will be honest and say I do not have one, and I do not listen to them. In fact, I recently spoke to someone who does produce one, and when I asked if she listened to them herself, she said no!

Newsletters

If you talk to any marketing expert, they will tell you to get clients emails and create a database so that you can email them newsletters. Before doing so, I recommend that you familiarise yourself with the General Data Protection Regulation (GDPR), see *Notetaking*. You must allow your clients to opt-out of email marketing if they wish to.

A newsletter will only be read if it is relevant to them, has interesting information, and it is fun. The only newsletter I enjoyed receiving was from a dress stylist who would tell me the latest up and coming colours and trends for the season. It is not that I am a great follower of fashion, but I loved the flow and feel of the newsletter. Give your client's something of value.

You do not want to fill your client's inbox with a bombardment of emails. They will just switch off. Keep your newsletters monthly or even quarterly, limit them to one page and make them easy to read.

Notes and Ideas

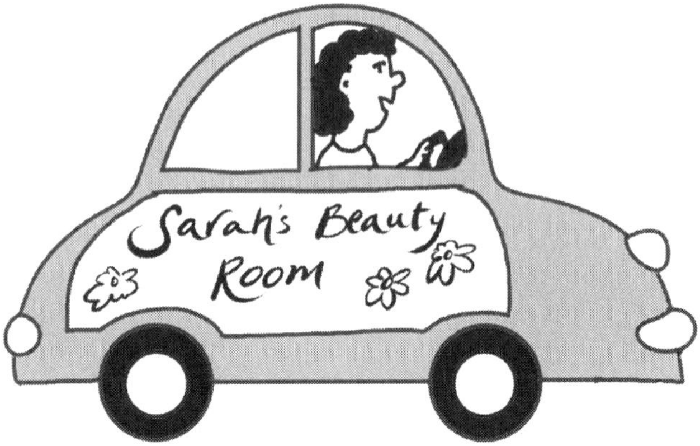
Sarah's Beauty
Room

Car Signage

This is a great way to advertise. Who hasn't sat in a queue of traffic and read the sign on the back of the car in front? However, the chances are you will be driving around town or overtaking on the motorway, so your sign needs to be big, bold and above all clear about what you do.

I've seen so many cars or vans saying things like www.I canhelpyou.com and nothing else. I can help you do what? If there is nothing else on the vehicle indicating what they do, you will not be inclined to find out.

When passing cars, you will have a split second to see the signage, so think carefully about what you are saying. "Lulu's Boutique" could mean anything from pampered dog coats to nail art. State exactly what is on offer. "Lulu's Beauty Therapy" is a straight statement to what you do.

Put this on along with your website,

www.lulusbeautytherapy.co.uk

and hopefully, people will remember it, because your website address matches your company name.

Most people have internet access and will look you up before picking up the phone. They won't remember your telephone number or be able to note it down while driving, but they may remember your business name. You can include your telephone number if you have space on your vehicle, but make sure your company name comes first.

Notes and Ideas

House signage

I was lucky enough to put a sign, much like a pub sign on the side of the road advertising my business. This was a great form of subliminal advertising as cars were driving past night and day.

Sadly, after 12 years of free advertising, I was told by the council to take it down, so I took it down and put it up in my front garden.

I also have a sign as you turn into my drive, and another on the house. All of them make it easy for my clients to find me.

WHO IS YOUR IDEAL CLIENT?

Have a look at the section entitled *Become an expert*. This ties in with knowing your ideal client. This will come with experience, and sometimes you just must go with the flow and find your niche.

Once you know your ideal client, you can then target your marketing specifically towards that audience.
There is no point in saying, everyone. Not everyone is your ideal client.

GIVEAWAYS

Everyone uses a pen, and this makes it the perfect gift to give to a client on their first appointment. If pens are not your thing, give them a sample of your products if you use them. Giving your client something extra makes them feel special.

I give new clients a business card, leaflet, and a pen. I make my own angel cards and have them in a bowl for my clients to choose one after every appointment. If they are spiritual, I call it an angel card, if they are not, I call it a card for guidance. Either way, they love them. If the client is a child, I offer one to them and one to their parent.

If you sell products, you could give them another product as a sample. If your client has spent over a certain amount on skin products, you could provide them with a hand cream sample on their next appointment. The sample could be an aromatherapy blend or a sachet of the cream you use in your therapy room.

Giveaways are great at fairs but be careful not to give away too much. The idea is you want to gain a client from it. You don't want to give them to someone who is just minesweeping the tables to see what they can hoover up for free.

Create your own prize draw

Ask for contact details and put them in a bowl. The winner will receive either a prize or a therapy session. Keep it small - give away a facial rather than a full body massage.

Sometimes fair organisers ask for a raffle prize. I have learnt over the years that you are better off giving something that relates to your business rather than a therapy session. Give a set of body creams or a mini pamper set with your business card and leaflet in it. People that win prizes will come for their prize and leave.

The clients that speak to you on the day and are genuinely interested in your products and/or services are your best potential clients.

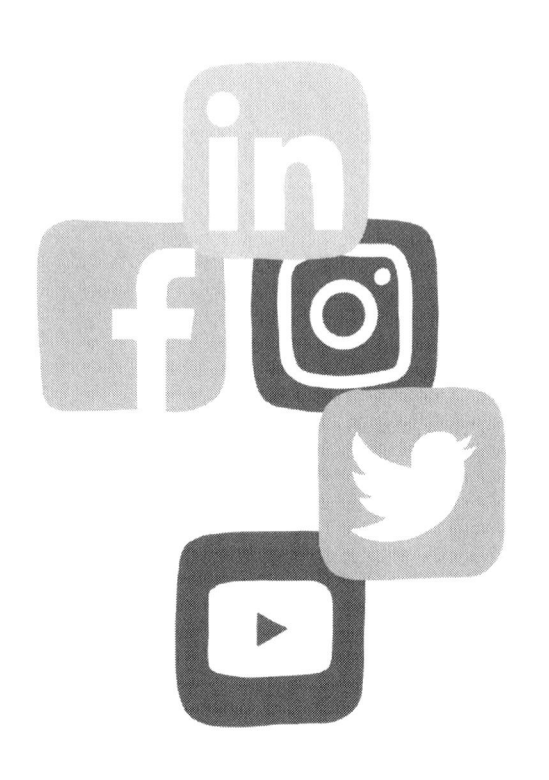

SOCIAL MEDIA

Social media is an excellent way of connecting with people so that they can get to know, like and trust you. You can either love it or hate. Do learn to embrace and use it because it's not going away. Find out what works best for your therapy. I use Facebook, LinkedIn, Twitter, and Instagram. Get to know them well and be consistent with your postings.

There is no point in you posting five times in one hour and then nothing for the rest of the week.

Get yourself on some courses or workshops and learn how to use them effectively.

Use a social media buffer so you can create loads of content and then use a scheduler to post them.

Keep it professional. Potential clients will see what you have been up to at the weekend. Make sure you have no embarrassing photographs on there, and no political or religious rants either.

You have a code of conduct in your line of work; this also applies to social media.

Social media is growing, and you cannot be on every platform effectively. Pick one or two and get to know them well.

Notes and Ideas

MIND
BODY
SPIRIT
FAIR
HERE TODAY!

FAIRS

The type of therapy you provide will influence what type of fairs you do.

Places you could try are:

> - Mind Body Spirit fairs
> - School fetes
> - Wedding fairs
> - Baby Shows
> - Private tasters
> - Pamper evenings
> - Natural living show
> - Wellbeing shows
> - Fashion shows

When you do, your own taster parties think about how much you would like to earn. You need to cover your costs, petrol, money and doing evening work. How many clients can you see in an evening? I would aim for a minimum of six and a maximum of 9. Charge for a mini 20-minute session. Price it at just above a third of your usual hourly rate.

Many people take a laptop so that they can have a presentation running on their stall. However, be aware that you cannot always be present to keep an eye on it. You could be on a bathroom break, working on a client, or talking to a potential client and you will not always have someone to cover your stall for you.

A cheaper alternative is to set up a photo presentation and then load it on to a digital photo frame. It is on a loop and draws people to your stall.

Another great thing I'd recommend is having lights on your stall. I have small battery lights that I put in a colourful mosaic vase and this works well.

Pop up banners are great. Make sure you have your writing on the top half, as they often must be placed behind your table. Think about the wording too - what will draw your client in? A banner that says, "Are you looking to improve your life?" will have much more impact than "Tracy Montgomery – Homeopath."

If you are taking electrical equipment, make sure you take extension leads. Hazard tape and scissors are handy for securing your cables firmly to the floor to prevent any trips. Get your electrical equipment PAT (Portable Appliance Testing) tested. You can either ask an electrician to do this for you, or the fair organizer may know of someone.

Ensure you make a tick list and put it in your fair bag. To help you, I have created one for you to download here, print off and keep it in your fair bag or box.

https://www.thespiritwithin.co.uk/the-secret-to-being-a-good-therapist-book/

Fair List

- Business cards
- Couch
- Diary
- Disposable aprons
- Disposable gloves
- Extension lead
- Face masks
- Fleece
- Giveaways
- Hand sanitiser
- Hazard tape
- Incense (if allowed)
- Laptop or device to showcase your work
- Lighters
- Ornaments
- Paper
- Pens
- Pop up banners
- Posters
- Powder / oil / creams
- Raffle prize for the organiser (keep it small, e.g., a mini facial)
- Scissors
- Small handbag/satchel to keep phone etc in
- Stock
- Tablecloth
- Towels
- Wet wipes
- Lastly, do remember your lunch and a flask!

Keep hydrated at fairs, especially if you are in a hot marquee in the summer. They are very tiring, and you are on your feet all day. However, they do get you out and meeting people who are interested in finding out about your therapy.

Keep to your catchment area unless you work online. If you are going to a fair located thirty miles away, are those clients going to travel to see you?

A word on your lunch... stay on your stall to eat your lunch. The minute you leave, you will find someone looking at it. The same goes for eating. The minute you open your lunch and take the first bite; someone will turn up and ask you a question. Keep your lunch small and bite-size. That way, you can sneak the occasional bite when there is a lull in the day.

At fairs you can either be flat out busy or twiddling your thumbs. Do keep your mobile phone watching to a minimum. If you are sitting there with your head down looking at your phone potential clients will just walk on by.

Depending on space, try and sit on the edge of your stall so you can stand and engage with people as they approach your stall. You will appear open and more responsive to their needs rather than sitting behind a table creating a barrier between you.

Notes and Ideas

NETWORKING

Networking is really growing in popularity, and you could probably go to a different networking group every day three times a day if you wanted to. When you find a group, you think you would like to join, take into consideration these things:

Location

While you may be prepared to drive a round trip of 40 miles to a networking group, ask yourself is it likely my clients will do the same? Even though some of the groups sound appealing, I stick to my catchment area of 10 miles from my home. Most clients will say they chose you because you are local to them.

Business or pleasure

Ask yourself what you are getting from networking and whether you are happy with that. Networking may not necessarily bring business, but it may make you feel a part of a larger organization and provide a sense of connection with others. A colleague once said that whilst it was lovely to meet up with familiar faces at networking, they are not your friends, you are here to get business and so are they. That said, many do become friends who may not use your services but will happily recommend your business.

Affordability

Some groups are free, some are pay-as-you-go, some charge a yearly fee, and others charge an annual fee plus a joining fee AND a fee for lunch or breakfast. What can you afford? Are your costs being covered? Ideally, you want to be making a profit from your investment. Also, ask yourself if you can afford the time out of your business. If you are filling your diary with networking dates, are you missing calls from prospective clients?

Sixty Second Pitch

Many groups ask you to stand up and deliver a sixty-second pitch. Do prepare this. Write a script the day before and time yourself, then adjust your script accordingly. Don't wing it. You will either say too much or not enough.

Start with your name, company and what you can do for your audience. You could use a case study or tell a story, but remember you only have one minute.

Ask for the business and remember to promote any relevant special offers. E.g., "I have a special offer this month on back, neck and shoulder massages. I'm looking for anyone who's suffering because they've been hunched over their computer all day and would like their tension released from their muscles".

Keep to your sixty seconds. There will be plenty of businesspeople in the room, and their time is precious. When you go over time, you are robbing them of their time, and they will be bored with your spiel and even resentful.

Stand up straight and talk confidently. Look at the back of the room above your audience's heads and occasionally make eye contact by sweeping your eyes from one side of the room to the other. Keep your hands empty and open, or if you need a script in front of you, hold it firmly, so you are not waving it about in front of you. RELAX. You know what you are talking about.

Tagline

It is worth having a tagline for your business. A tagline is a phrase or a slogan that you can use in advertising. It should be memorable and catchy.

I have never changed the name of my business. My first tagline was "Let your healing begin at The Spirit Within". Later, I changed it to "If you never go within, you go without". Say it every time you give your pitch, and your audience will recognize it and start saying it back to you.

Be consistent and always use the same tagline, both verbally and on your literature, website, and social media.

Speaker Pitch

I strongly suggest that you put yourself forward to be a speaker of the week or month. You may find this rather daunting but get yourself out of your comfort zone and do it! The more you do it, the better at it you will become. Give a small demonstration if you can. Offer an incentive to book a session with you, but do not feel obliged to discount your services. For example, you can have a free hand massage if you book a facial.

Dress

Dress smartly. You are representing your business. 55% of your communication is in your body language, so stand up straight and look smart. If you look good, you will feel good. Scruffy dress = scruffy attitude.

Business cards and leaflets

Always have your business cards and/or leaflets ready, always. There is nothing worse than engaging with someone, who is so interested in your business that they ask for your card and you do not have any. I recently met someone I wanted to hook up with and asked for her card. She said she did not do business cards and told me I would find her?! Do you think I tried? Make it easy for your potential clients to contact you.

You may be able to put your cards on a separate table or on the breakfast/dinner table you are sitting at. If people ask for your card, make sure you have them ready rather than fumbling about in the bottom of your handbag or briefcase. Hand them the card horizontally, facing them. This way, they can immediately read it without having to turn it around to see it.

If they do not ask for your card, you can say "May I give you my card?".

You can get caught up with someone who is just telling you all about their business, and they are not a potential customer. If this happens, you can excuse yourself without being rude by saying "It's been lovely talking with you, I've just seen someone I need to talk to" and walk away.

Other therapists

Unfortunately, as therapists, we tend to gravitate to likeminded souls and invariably, we end up sitting next to other therapists. Make a mental note to acknowledge them and then sit somewhere else. You may be pitching for the same business.

Move around

Human beings are creatures of habit. We tend to sit in the same place, at the same table and talk to the same people, week in, week out. It is best to move around and hop from table to table. It is natural to head for the people you know, so take yourself out of your comfort zone and talk to people you do not know. Meeting and connecting with new people are what networking is all about and, as the same group of people attend regularly, you'll get to know everyone eventually.

121

If you meet a potential client or equally, you are interested in someone else's business, make sure you arrange a follow-up meeting after the networking meeting. If you both have time, have a coffee straight after the meeting. Be proactive. If their schedules are busy, arrange for a coffee straight after the next networking meeting.

Clients in the room

Once you have made some contacts and they are coming to you for therapy it is up to them to tell others that they see you, not you. Acknowledge them at the meeting. Talk to them as you usually would but do not discuss their therapy or their next appointment in front of other people unless they choose to.

Be present

If you sit on your mobile phone in a networking meeting, others will notice. It is different if you have a sick child and you may receive a call, or you keep it on for an elderly relative but keep it on silent. Excuse yourself from the meeting quietly if you need to. Other than that, keep it turned off. Do not sit texting or checking emails during the meeting or presentations – it's just rude!

Photography

When I am chatting to someone or eating my breakfast, I don't want someone pointing a mobile phone in my face to take my photograph without my permission. This is for their own self-promotion so that they can post the pictures on social media and then use your name and tag you and others to say where they are and what they are doing. I avoid such people. My website has my practice address on it, and I do not want the fact that I am sitting in a hotel somewhere to be posted on social media. Be mindful of this if you do this. Ask permission first.

If you take photographs, take them of the venue or the back of the audience facing the presentation screen.

Keep calm and carry on

Attend your chosen networking groups regularly. You cannot expect people to choose your business after meeting you once. I heard one man moaning that networking did not work for him after having attended just three meetings. You must attend consistently for people to know, like and trust you.

But also know when to stop. I did the same networking group for two years, and I covered my costs and made a profit. I left the group as I figured everyone who was ever going to come for therapy had called me and done so. Know when to move on. There are plenty of other groups from which to choose. You'll get known if you switch from group to group and it won't look good as you are not committing to any particular group. Also, no one will get to know, like and trust you if you are only there for one or two meetings.

Minesweepers

There are some individuals that mine sweep the business card table. I have even seen people coming in and taking all the cards, then making an excuse they could not stay. Later, members get a newsletter or an email, saying "further to our chat today." Such behaviour does not create a positive impression with fellow business owners.

Social media

When you have exchanged business cards with someone connect with them on social media. Add them to your personal and your business page. Get to know them better. Sometimes therapy can be a slow feed. I have had clients call me two years after they first picked up my business card.

WORKSHOPS

These are a great way of earning extra income. You can run regular workshops, or you can run them at certain times of the year when your diary is quiet.

There are a variety of meeting places available. Some therapists use pubs. In the public area, it's free, or they may charge for a separate meeting room. It would be helpful to ask your attendees to buy drinks and lunch there if it's an all-day event.

Schools rent their rooms out in the evening or at weekends. Ensure that you can provide drinks and a few biscuits.

Community halls can be suitable, but they can sometimes be cold and typically take some setting up. Bear that in mind if you are demonstrating massages.

If you have the room, you can run workshops at your home. Keep it professional by ensuring that your family are at work or school. Also be mindful of animals you may have and settle them down in another room.

GIVING PRESENTATIONS

People are more afraid of giving a presentation than dying. The more presentations you give, the easier it becomes. The way I look at it is they have come to listen to you, and there is nobody in the room that wants to see you fail.

Presentations are a great way to boost your confidence and demonstrate your expertise.

The first presentation I gave was to a room of 200 people. It was at a conference, and a speaker picked me out and asked me to help him in his presentation. He gave me a microphone and script, and he explained that I was interacting with him.

When I left the auditorium, people came up and congratulated me before telling me how they could not have done it.

Once you settle into public speaking, you may find you enjoy it. You can use props, ask your audience to participate and get your audience to ask questions.

Presentations are an excellent opportunity for you to educate your audience about your therapy and for you to give out your business cards, leaflets, and giveaways and of course, speak to potential clients.

Places you could present to include:

- Women's Institute
- The Rotary club
- Sailing club (you can tell I live near the sea!)
- Golf club
- Schools
- Universities
- Mind Body Spirit fairs
- Health and wellbeing fairs
- Green fairs
- Doctors
- Hospitals
- Hospices
- Dentists
- Chemists
- Networking groups
- Ladies that lunch clubs
- Corporate companies
- Health shops
- Positive living groups
- Private taster parties

Notes and Ideas

WALK THE TALK

If you are a chiropractor, keep yourself in good shape and check your posture regularly. We want beauticians to make us look good. We go to them for a pamper and want to come out with a lovely fresh manicure or pedicure. It is not a good look if the beautician has no makeup on, with hair scrunched up and chipped nails.

We all forget from time to time that it is important to "walk the talk". We can spend all day advising clients to drink more water, and we do not do it ourselves.

Once, when I was suffering from a cold, a fellow aromatherapist asked me if I was using eucalyptus and tea tree essential oils to help clear it. I replied "no!". Even though I am a qualified aromatherapist, I had forgotten about the benefits of using my own oils.

Think about it. What you are doing, or are recommending for your clients and ask yourself, am I doing the same? I know of so many therapists who say to me that they are always busy looking after others, and yet they never make time for themselves.

WALK THE TALK, make time!

Around October I buy my diary for the following year. The first thing I do is block out my holidays. Usually, I take a week off every three months, apart from summer, when I take two weeks off. However, in the first three years of trading, I did not take any holiday.

Do this, and you will, like I did, suffer from therapist burn out. It is essential to look after yourself. Healer, heal thyself. You can then be at your optimum to help your clients. If your clients come in moaning, they are so tired you do not want to be there feeling the same as them.

You can book in for regular treatments with salons that do not know what you do so you can chill out and not talk "shop", or you can look after yourself by swapping therapy with your peers or some that charge "mate's rates".

Notes and Ideas

SECURITY

It is your responsibility to ensure that you and your belongings are safe. We would all like to think we know our clients, but when you have a busy practice, and you discover, at the end of the day that your purse or wallet is missing, how will you know who took it?

Put your purse/wallet, car keys, mobile phone, handbag etc. out of sight. Put them in a locked drawer, a cupboard, or, if you are working from home, in another room.

If you have a laptop, PC, or iPad in your room, make sure you screen lock it before leaving a client alone in your therapy room. The same rule goes for your client's notes and diary. I once came back to my room after getting a client a glass of water only to find her going through my/her records. If you need to leave the room, either take them with you or lock them away before you leave the room.

With experience, you'll be able to hone your skills at vetting your clients on the telephone. Many clients these days prefer to email you and will book an appointment without you having spoken to them. I recommend that they phone first so that you can assess how likely they are to turn up, whether they are committed to the therapy being offered and whether they are nervous or not.

Equally, you may not like their attitude or feel uncomfortable taking them on as a client. If this is the case, you can say you are not the therapist for them and suggest they call someone else. You can also warn your peers that this person may be calling them next (without naming names of course) and advise them of your concerns. Or you may like to refer them to another therapist.

Some therapists only work with same-sex clients. Remember, you are the boss, and you make the rules. If you feel uncomfortable working with a client, finish the session, do not rebook saying you are not the therapist for them. If you know a therapist, you can refer them to then by all means do. But you may find that you do not want to recommend them to anyone, in which case, say "I am sorry I don't know of anyone."

You may rebook a client and have an odd feeling about seeing them again. Trust in your gut feeling. As therapists, we want to help and care for everyone, but putting yourself in danger or even feeling uneasy is just not worth it, either for you or the other clients you see that day.

I had a very heated discussion with a young lady in my therapy room one day. She had received a massage. She wanted a back, neck and shoulder massage. Part of my routine is to massage the client's arms. I took the towels off her arms and not only did she look anorexic she also self-harmed. I had exposed her and her secret. After the massage, I told her I would leave the room while she dressed. When I returned, she was angry and refused to pay me. I addressed this by saying she had booked me for a service, and I had provided that service, so she now needed to pay me. After a heated discussion, I opened the door and told her to leave. She was threatening me by saying she would give me a bad review. When I checked out her details, her telephone number and address were fake. I never heard from her again.

I say this not to frighten you, but to point out that you will, occasionally, come across unreasonable clients. I would not say shouting at a client is the best way to handle this situation, but when confronted with non-payment and a desire to undermine my services, I stood firm and told her to leave. We know the saying "the customer is always right", but we all know some people just try it on.

If a client tries to get intimate with you, set the boundaries. Tell them this is inappropriate behaviour and ask them to leave. You are the therapist, and they are the client. It is your business, and you do not allow this kind of conduct. Some therapists say they do not take payment in such circumstances, but why should you lose your money? I have always charged them for wasting my time.

For female therapists, you may prefer to have male clients only when they have been referred to you by an existing client, e.g., brother, husband, or father. If you are talking to a new male client for a massage, I always ask "Have you had a massage before?" Then I ask what kind? If they say Swedish body massage or aromatherapy, I would the ask them to elaborate. How did they feel? If they ask if you do a massage with extras or ask if you do it naked then hang up.

You can install CCTV around your property, but for confidentially you would not install it in your therapy room. Notify your clients that you have CCTV installed for your and their security in your terms and conditions.

LADIES/GENTS WHO LATTE

When you work for yourself, you can work as little or as much as you want. Some therapists like work to fit around the school run, some like to see only a few clients a week, others want a full-time profession to pay the mortgage. Whichever business model you prefer, make sure you take time off. Book your days off and meet up with colleagues and friends over a coffee or lunch.

If you were working in an office, you would be talking with your mates about last night's Britain's Got Talent, but this is not something you talk about with your clients.

Being a therapist can be lonely and very isolating, so make sure that you have regular breaks in your day. Remember, you are the boss!

WORKING HOURS

You now work for yourself so you can kiss goodbye to your 9 to 5 job, overtime, paid holidays, and sick pay.

On the plus side, you set your own hours, so yes, you can work 9 to 5 should you wish to. Being self-employed means that you may find yourself replying to text messages or emails at 9.30 pm on a Saturday night when the "nine to fivers" have long forgotten about work. You'll be updating your website or doing your tax return on a Sunday morning too. BUT, again, it's your choice! You choose the hours you want to work.

Choose your late nights. What is the latest appointment time you are prepared to accept, and whether you want to work on a Saturday or not? Usually, I keep my Saturday mornings clear for my London clients. It's a long commute to Hampshire, and I do not want to be working at 9.30 pm during the week.

HEALTH AND SAFETY

Pets

You may love your dog and think it's great to take your pet to work, or if you work from home allow it in your therapy room, but not all of your clients will be pet lovers. Even if they have animals themselves, they are paying for you to give them your full attention and give excellent service, not to have your attention distracted by a dog barking or a cat meowing.

Some of your clients may have asthma, allergies or breathing problems, which you will only find out about once they arrive. Rest assured they will not return to you.

I have cats. They are never allowed in my therapy room. Some clients can be so sensitive that they suffer from traces of pet fur that can linger on your clothes. To avoid this, I have a uniform which I wear for my holistic work.

Covid-19

As I am writing this book in 2020, it seems appropriate that I mention Covid-19 and how it affected my own and many other therapy businesses. We are in the well-being profession, and while we could remain calm and reassuring to our clients after receiving such devastating news, we had the same fears and anxieties as everyone else. It brings home to us, even more so, the importance of our health.

I have already covered the importance of telling your clients that you are going to wash your hands, but this could also include hand sanitizing, face masks, and even gowning up. I have, for many years, worn a face mask for doing holistic work on any client who has told me they have a sniffle or are getting over a cold. Remember you need to protect yourself and keep yourself well as well as looking after your clients.

I cleanse the chair, couch and the therapy room between clients and disinfect it all at the end of every day. Include the bathroom if clients have used it.

Other areas to consider:

- Front doorbell or knocker
- Handles, handrails, and bannisters
- Lift buttons and light switches
- Toilet and sink area
- Chairs in a waiting area
- Pens or mobile device screens
- Payment terminal
- Computer keyboard and mouse

Finally, have (PPE) personal protective equipment, e.g., disposable face masks and gloves available for your clients if they require them. You can charge them for these or add them into your fees to cover the costs.

Things clients use

I used to give my clients a glass of water after every therapy session. I found I had so many glasses to wash up at the end of the day that I changed it to disposable plastic cups which I buy in bulk. Because of the impact of plastic on the planet, I will change them to paper cups in the future.

I have flannels in the bathroom for my clients to dry their hands on which means I must wash these at the end of the day. I will change this to paper towels that can be disposed of in a pedal bin and emptied at the end of the day.

Protection

I always recommend protecting yourself every day. There are several ways to do this, depending on your beliefs. You can imagine yourself inside an egg of golden light; covered with a long-hooded cloak, or inside a pyramid of mirrors and visualise any negativity will bounce off and away from you. For men, I recommend a suit of armour; they seem to like this one. For children, they could imagine dressing up as their favourite television character or superhero.

Nurses and doctors have been doing it for years, putting on their white coat of protection or scrubs.

When I started, I would only wear my uniform to treat clients and then change afterwards. It mentally helped me to know that work has finished. Nowadays, however, I prefer not to wear a uniform, so it helps to go through these mental protection exercises.

Sometimes when we are working with someone, and you start feeling tired or get a sick feeling in your solar plexus, you can mentally quickly put on your protection. It really does work!

We are open to people's emotions. You know what it feels like when you walk into a room where someone has recently had a row. We say you could have cut the atmosphere with a knife. How would you feel if you went into a room and sat in a chair or laid on a couch where a person had been sobbing?

After a client has left, I scoop up their energy from around the room, and then sweep down myself and put it in a box on my window seal and ask the angels to take care of it.

For hands-on therapy, go and wash your hands mentally, saying to yourself that you are washing away their negativity.

If you feel particularly drained, take off your shoes and socks and stamp your feet to ground yourself, preferably in the garden if you can.

Grounding means getting yourself out of your head back into your body very quickly. (This is another useful tool that you can use with clients if they are feeling spaced out after their therapy).

You and your room are then ready for your next client. Do this again at the end of the day, and you'll be surprised how energised you feel.

Disability Access

It is up to you to do all you can as a business owner to provide a welcoming environment for **all** of your customers.

If your therapy room is upstairs, are you able to see clients downstairs if needed?

If you cannot provide disability access to your property or treatment room, can you rent a room elsewhere to provide a service for your client?

I rented a room in a chiropractor's practice which was upstairs. It did seem ludicrous to me that clients with back problems would have to drag themselves upstairs and then after their treatment struggle to get back down the stairs. I asked how they would treat someone in a wheelchair? The reply was "We wouldn't".

In my book, this is discrimination, so I pulled my therapy business away from them.

Fire extinguisher

If you are using essential oils, burners, waxing equipment, ear candles, candles, or incense, you should keep a fire extinguisher in your room. They do have an expiry date on them so make sure it is in date. Familiarise yourself on how to use it.

In the event of a fire

If your clients undress for their therapy, keep a clean bathrobe on the back of your therapy room door. In the event of a fire, they can grab this and leave the building as quickly as possible, with their dignity intact.

First aid

Many years ago, I went to a friend's house for Reiki. As I lay on the couch dozing, I suddenly became aware of her hands getting heavier and heavier. Suddenly she lurched forward over me and then flew backwards hitting the floor.

I jumped off the couch to find her laid on the floor with her eyes wide open. I thought she was dead.

I then ran around the house, trying to locate her husband, whom I found in the garden. By the time we got back to her, she was slowly coming to, having fainted. I thought, what if this was a client in my therapy room? Soon after, I booked myself on a first aid course. It is well worth having this training not just for your clients but for yourself and your family. The certificate is valid for three years, and you can put it in your CPD folder. (See Continuous Professional Development CPD).

Keep an easily assessable first aid kit in your therapy room and an accident book.

Check the dates on your first aid kit. They last approximately three years.

The accident book can be just a small book that says accident book on it. I keep mine with my first aid kit. You will need to enter the date and time of the accident, what happened, the name of the client and who was there at the time. This must then be signed by both parties and the injured party must have a copy. This may be used in evidence for any claim against you.

THINGS TO CLAIM FOR

There are many things you can claim for as expenses against your business. Some are relatively obvious, some less so. Surprisingly, many therapists do not think about claiming for things like tissues, toilet paper or soap powder. To make your life easier, I have created a checklist which you can download here, print off and keep in your expenses tin or folder as a weekly reminder. I always tend to ask myself can I claim for this when I am out shopping. If I can, then I pay for it using my business bank account.

https://www.thespiritwithin.co.uk/the-secret-to-being-a-good-therapist-book/

Expenses List

Uniform	**Therapy room supplies**
Aprons	Accident book
Bag (if mobile)	Anti-viral foam
Cleaning uniform	Antibacterial wipes
Dresses	Bathrobe (back of door)
Shoes	Bin
Tops	Bin liners
Trousers	Books
	Candles
	Chairs
Therapy room	Couch covers
Air conditioning unit	Couch roll
Blind/curtains	Desk
Books	Disposable facial masks
Carpet	Disposable gloves
CCTV signs	First aid kit
CCTV/Alarm	Flannels
Chairs	Fleece blankets
Couch	Folders
Desk	Hand sanitiser
Fire extinguisher	Incense
Lamps	Incense holder
Lampshades	Kitchen towel
Light dimmer	Lighters
Music	Paper/plastic cups
No smoking signs	Petty cash slips
Ornaments	Petty cash tin
Paint	Pillows
	Plastic folders

Pictures
Recording equipment
Rent
Secure filing cabinet
Sound system
Vase/flowers
Water dispenser

Supplies for your business e.g.
Acupuncture needles
Cotton wool
Ear candles
Essential oils
Nail polish
Nail polish remover
Oils/creams/powder

Office
Bin
Blind/curtains
Bookcase

Receipt book
Room spray
Small table
Towels
Toys

Advertising
Advertisements papers/magazines
Banners
Business cards
Compliment slips
Flyers
Gift vouchers
Leaflets
Magazines
Marketing agent
Papers
Pop up banners
Practice signage
Press release agent
Road signage
Social media agent
Social media fees

Books
Carpet
CCTV signs
CCTV/Alarm
Chairs
Clock
Computer
Crosscut shredder
Desk
Fire extinguisher
Laminator
Lamps
Lampshades
No smoking signs
Ornaments
Paint
Pictures
Printer
Secure filing cabinet
Telephone
Vase/flowers

Stationery
Cards
Diary
Envelopes
Files

Supervision/CPD
Costs per meeting
Costs per year
Lunch/drinks
Travelling to/from

Volunteering
Costs of free therapy
Creams/oils
Lunch/drinks
Other supplies used
Travelling to/from your business

Networking
Cost of online conferencing software
Costs per annum
Costs per meeting
Lunch/breakfast/drinks
Travelling costs to/from

Courses/workshops
Conferences
Course
Lunch/drinks

Laminator sheets
Notepads
Pens
Printer cartridges
Printer paper
Writing paper

Bathroom
Paper towels
/flannels
Soap
Toilet rolls
Towels
Washing powder
Waste bin

Car
Signage
Check out HRMC website every year for % allowance to claim travelling, to/from clients, networking, fairs etc.

Seminars
Supervision
Talks
Travelling to/from
Workshop

Holistic Fairs/beauty shows
Chair
Extension leads
Forms
Giveaways
Hazard tape
Lamp
Lunch/drinks
Mileage
Pens
Portable couch
Portable couch cover
Stand fee
Storage boxes
Table
Tablecloth
Travelling to/from
Trolley

Utilities	**Yearly fees**
Broadband %	Accountant
Electric %	Electronic diary system
Gas %	Insurance
Landline %	Professional memberships
Mobile phone %	
Water %	
% work out amount used for your practice	

Complimentary Therapies

You can claim for the complimentary therapies you give. Put a petty slip in your expenses for the regular price you would charge for your treatment.

Telephone

If you are using your mobile number for business, then it is no longer your "personal" mobile. Clients can, (and they will) call or text you any time night or day unless you educate them otherwise. However, you'll still have clients who think it is acceptable to text or call you at 9.30 pm on a Saturday night or a bank holiday.

You could buy a second mobile and use it just for work, but then you have to remember to switch it on, check it and carry it around with you, which all seems a bit outdated.

You could give your clients your landline number if you work from home and screen calls out of working hours before answering them. You can then decide when to return the call. Would you call your dentist or doctor out of hours and expect a response? Set the same boundaries for your clients and return their call at 9.00 am on Monday.

There are systems you can put in place, so the telephone number on your website is different from your private number. You could have an 0800 number, and you can even pay for additional campaign numbers.

Having separate phone numbers for each advertising campaign allows you to monitor the effectiveness of each so that you can see which advert works best. It all depends on how far you want to go and how much you want to pay.

Mileage

The cost of the mileage you claim covers your petrol and wear and tear on your car. Check the mileage allowance every year when you start your new tax year as the amount you can claim does change from time to time. Check it out here:

https://www.gov.uk

ACCOUNTANT

I have never had an accountant. Nowadays, it is surprisingly easy to maintain your own accounts. Of course, it depends on the size and scale of your business and whether you feel comfortable doing your accounts yourself.

I do know of therapists who have accountants, and they say they know ways of saving them money on different purchases. I'm sceptical and would question whether the savings generated outweigh the accountant's fees?

TAX FORMS

When you first get started the idea of tax returns may fill you with horror, but they are surprisingly easy to complete. You can do them online at

https://www.gov.uk

There is plenty of help available online, or by telephone, so you do not need to struggle.

Notes and Ideas

CONTINUOUS PROFESSIONAL DEVELOPMENT (CPD)

If you have come from a corporate background as I have, you would have been so used to quarterly reviews, leading to yearly assessments. Nobody is doing this to you now, and it is up to you to ensure that you give the best therapy to your client that you can. Keep up to date with continuous professional development. It is good for you and your client. Keep a CPD folder to keep all your paperwork together.

If you belong to one of several professional memberships, they usually run courses or workshops. Book several a year. They do not necessarily have to be anything to do with what you are offering, as long as it's useful research.

Buy professional books and magazines as all of these are claimable. Keep up to date with the latest trends. Even if it is not something, you currently offer, you need to be aware of it, should a client contact you asking for it. Meeting up with fellow therapists all count towards your CPD and can be logged.

Workshops, talks and peer group supervision provide you with payment slips or certificates of attendance to put in your folder. Writing for magazines, newspapers, or a book are all eligible CPD points too.

Your insurance company or your professional membership may ask to see your records. Be prepared and have them ready.

Here's a list of items that count towards your CPD points. You may like to photocopy or type them and keep in your CPD folder.

Continuous Professional Development List

Courses	Get a certificate of attendance or keep a copy of the invoice
Workshops	Get a certificate of attendance or keep a copy of the invoice
Magazine/newspaper articles	Keep a copy
Attending talks	Keep the email of the outline of the talk and a receipt
Giving talks	Keep a copy of your talk
Giving workshops	Keep a copy of your workshop
Books and magazines	Write a review of a book you have read and say what you

	learnt from it
Meeting fellow therapists	Write a review of what you discussed (refrain from using client names) and what you learnt from it
Peer group supervision	Write a review of what you discussed (refrain from using client names) and what you learnt from it. Keep a copy of the invoice.
121 supervision	Write a review of what you discussed (refrain from using client names) and what you learnt from it. Keep a copy of the invoice.

Notes and Ideas

TESTIMONIALS

People buy from people. These days, reading reviews and testimonials is seen as an essential part of researching a therapist.

Ask your clients for referrals. When they have finished their course of therapy with you, give them some business cards and ask them to refer people to you.

There is no better advertising than word of mouth. Ask your clients to post good reviews on social media and Google. Ask them to email you a testimonial. You can use these anonymously on your website, leaflets, and social media or with their name if you obtain their permission.

Just before they finish their therapy, send them an email with all the links for this. Make it easy for them to respond.

If clients are enthusing about their therapy, ask them to put that in their testimonial.

I always use the client's words. Do not change them to suit you or your business. Be authentic.

PART TWO

HINTS AND TIPS FOR YOUR PRACTICE

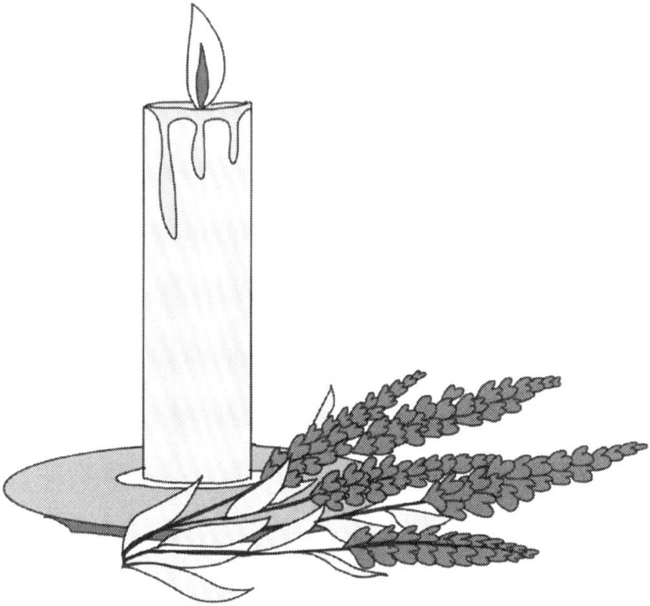

BEING A CONFIDENT MASSEUSE

My teacher taught me how to massage the complete body. Today, it seems that many schools miss out vital areas of the body. If you have not been taught a full body massage, I recommend that you study these additional areas. Doing so will dramatically enhance your client's massage experience.

Feet

I particularly love having my legs and feet massaged. Most people offer back, neck and shoulder massage as a short massage. For those clients who, like me, love to have their legs massage, why not provide a complete leg and foot massage. Bliss!

Face

Learn how to do a fabulous facial. You can then include this in your back, neck, and shoulder massage, or as a stand-alone treatment or add to your complete deluxe body massage.

Abdomen

The abdomen is a vital area that many students leave out of their massages.

Massaging the solar plexus is crucial for helping a client to relax. People tend to hold tension in their Solar Plexus (see Chakras). Massaging this area is a very soothing way to help your client unwind.

If a female client has menstrual problems, massaging the abdomen in a clockwise motion can be very nurturing. It can also aid clients with Irritable Bowel Syndrome (IBS), Ulcerative Colitis and Crohn's by easing a constipated bowel and getting things moving again. I always advise such clients to drink more water too.

Massage the "V"

I have received so many massages where the therapist is too scared to massage near the pelvic region. One of my male case studies said: "Thank goodness you massaged my whole leg, instead of just above the knee!" Inevitably, there will be times when you flick something you should not have but always act professionally. Say nothing and carry on.

Buttocks

Men usually hold tension in their shoulders, and women hold it their buttocks. Hacking and cupping this area will release this tightness, which in turn releases the hips. I particularly recommend buttocks being massaged for clients with endometriosis and other menstrual problems.

Finally, advise your clients to remember to release the tension in their buttocks whilst standing. Many people hold tension in this area without even realizing they are doing so.

Ears

Remember that we have reflexology points, not only on our feet but also on our hands, face, and ears. Why not include the ears when massaging the face? Doing so feels nurturing because many people massage their baby's ears when they are on the breast.

When you massage your first few clients, you may be worried that you are working on a near-naked body and are concerned about ensuring that you keep them adequately covered. Just remember your training and relax as much as possible. If you relax so will your client.

We have all experienced a time when we have inadvertently flicked a breast or a man's genitals during a treatment. How you deal with such situations defines your level of professionalism. Do not start apologising. Chances are the client is so relaxed they would not have even noticed, and by apologising, you have broken relaxation and rapport.

Just ignore it, and so they will too.

COLOUR THERAPY

Like a lot of holistic therapists years ago, I chose lilac as my colour scheme. It is a feminine, pretty colour.

My therapy room had a beige carpet with magnolia walls and lilac curtains. I had navy trousers with a lilac polo shirt with my company name on the breast.
Later, the walls became lilac. Now, for many years I am happy with pale green walls with dark wooden slated blinds and an emerald carpet.

You want to look nurturing and welcoming without being too clinical.

For you chiropractors with skeletons and body parts on display, you can still adapt your room to look softer.

I like to see what colour my clients are wearing when they first come for therapy. Depressed clients tend to wear black or dark colours. As the treatment progresses, it is lovely to see the transformation in them. As they start to feel better about themselves, you'll see their colours change, as will their skin tone.

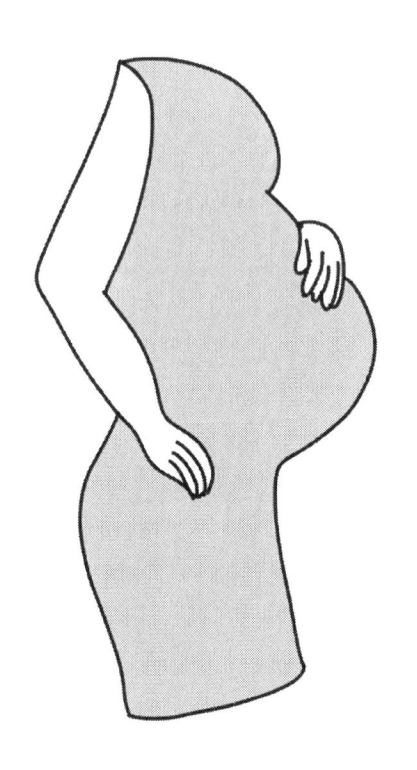

PREGNANCY

I only wanted to add this to put in top tips to help to bring a baby on.

Firstly, ask the client to go down on all fours and ask them to move their hips from side to side, like a dog wagging its tail.

Secondly, try side-walking down the stairs. For safety, make sure they have a bannister to hold.

Both exercises relieve any tension in the hips.

I would also recommend Reiki and reflexology points.

CHAKRAS

There are seven main chakras which are energy centres in the body.

Everything is made up of energy- plants, trees, animals, and us.

If a client has post-traumatic stress disorder (PTSD) or anxiety, I show them a simple technique which can help ground them very quickly.

Press your thumb firmly into the centre of the opposite palm and rotate.

This area is the reflexology point for the solar plexus. If something is affecting us, our solar plexus will be tense.

If you saw a horrendous car accident, your stomach would flip. If you have a presentation to give, you get butterflies. We get these "gut reactions" because we have brain cells in our stomach and so it's not surprising that we feel a reaction there when we are stressed.

Your clients can use their simple yet powerful technique anywhere. Beneath a school desk; on a plane, during a row with your mother-in-law. You can even use it when you are giving a presentation. It is so subtle that nobody will notice.

BREATHING

7/11 breathing is a beautiful way to calm down your clients and, as its name suggests, means breathing in for the count of seven, and then breathing out again for the count of eleven. This technique means they are exhaling more than they are inhaling.

Someone who is stressed may find this quite tricky because their breathing is usually shallow. If so, advise your client to shorten or lengthen it depending on their lung capacity. For children, I would use 4/8 breathing.

You can then introduce them to diaphragm breathing. If you look at a baby, they breathe from their diaphragm. As we age, we start to hold tension in our shoulders and breathe from the top of our lungs.

Ask your clients to take a deep breath, and you'll see their shoulders rise towards their ears.

The easiest way to get back to diaphragmatic breathing is to ask your clients to place their hands on their tummy, just below their rib cage, when they settle down for sleep. The tips of their fingers should be touching. When they inhale, they should notice their hands rising as their diaphragm expands. If they don't, they are not breathing correctly. It takes practice to break the habit but when they do, it's worth it. Always breathe from your diaphragm. This way, you are taking deeper breaths and using your full lung capacity, which energizes and de-stresses.

Notes and Ideas

CRYSTALS

The medicine box crystal is clear quartz. Clear quartz is the most powerful healing stone thought to work on any condition. It is said to protect against negativity and connects you to your higher self.

It is said to be particularly good for Fibromyalgia.

Clear quartz is excellent for office workers, and I recommend they put a piece in front of their computer to absorb negative emissions. It is also helpful for absorbing their own negativity.

Pink quartz is the crystal of love. It is good for opening your heart chakra and is especially suitable for infertility. It restores trust and harmony in relationships and promotes a deep connection with self-love and a feeling of peace.

I have a box of crystals that I use. Clients can hold them to ground themselves. They are also useful as gifts for clients. Ask them to choose one and then hold it during their healing session. They are also great to give to children as their "superpower" stone.

It is worth getting to know crystals and their different healing properties so that you feel comfortable with which to use and recommend.

Notes and Ideas

HEALING

If you are a therapist, then you are a healer. How many times have you entered your hairdressing salon feeling stressed only to leave feeling much better? It is not just because you have a new haircut; it is because you have spent time with a good listener and that they have been giving you healing through their hands as they have been touching your head.

It is so worth having qualified healing as part of your therapy practice. Even if you do not use it as one of your treatments, it will help enhance your work and your life on so many levels.

Healing is healing. Whether you call it Reiki, Munay- Ki, Shamanic or spiritual, we are all tapping into the universal love, and that is such a powerful tool.

AFFIRMATIONS

Affirmations work. I usually make a few suggestions and then ask my clients to come up with their own statements which will be more meaningful and compelling to them.

I advise them to look in the mirror every day and say their affirmations with conviction.

Here are a few:

I approve of myself

Clients with low self-esteem often find this affirmation hard at first.

I love you

Another potent affirmation that is often challenging for clients who have been in an abusive relationship.

I am safe, all is well

I get my clients who are prone to panic attacks to recite this while hugging themselves.

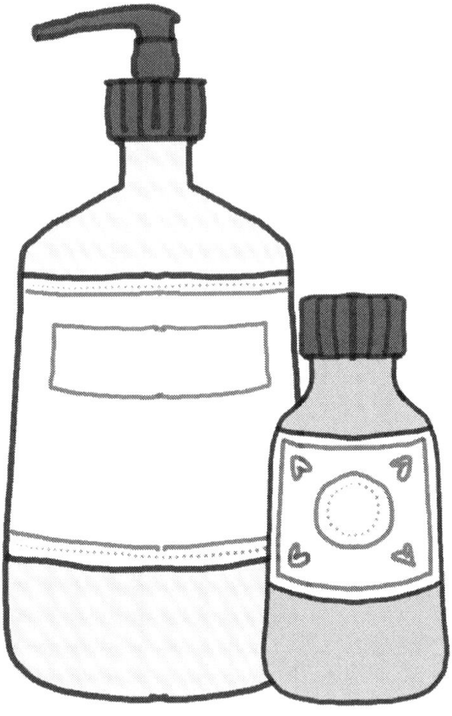

ESSENTIAL OILS

There are three main essential oils that are safe and useful to know. Use them on yourself, and you can then advise your clients about them.

Lavender

Lavender is the medicine cabinet of oils, one that every household should have. I call this one the anti-oil because of its powerful antioxidant, antimicrobial, sedative, calming and antidepressant properties. Lavender oil's benefits abound, and that's why it's been used, both cosmetically and therapeutically, for centuries.

Lavender is also versatile. I recommend just one drop on one side of your pillow at night to help you sleep. (Any more will keep you awake at night.) For a soothing bath, I recommend adding 6-8 drops of lavender oil to a capful of milk or Epsom salts as this helps to disperse the oils throughout the water. Put in the bath just before stepping in. Do not add while the water is still running as the oil will dissipate before you have stepped in. Use only 1-2 drops for babies or the elderly.

Lavender is an adaptogen which means it seems to be able to adapt to the needs of the person who uses it.

Tea Tree

A powerful antibacterial oil often used for skin infections, wound cleaning, and hand sanitization. It is also an excellent insect repellent, and you can use it for a whole host of different ailments from dandruff to psoriasis. Tea tree is widely available as an ingredient in creams, ointments, lotions, soaps, and shampoos. It can be used neat on spots or added to a carrier oil.

Mandarin

Of all the citrus oils, Mandarin essential oil is the sweetest and tends to be the most calming. It is considered very uplifting. I call it my "happy oil." Children love it, and it is a lovely oil to burn in your therapy room.

Ensure you always buy 100% essential oil. If it does not say 100%, you are likely to be buying part essential oil diluted with a cheap carrier oil.

Buy your carrier oil separately. I use often use grapeseed oil. A great one for facial skin is almond oil. (Always check for nut allergies.)

Although these essential and carrier oils are safe for external use, keep them out of the nursery and out of reach of children in your therapy room as they are harmful if ingested. If you are recommending oils to your clients make sure that you have a recognized aromatherapy qualification.

ABOUT THE AUTHOR

Deborah Lloyd has been a holistic therapist since 2000. Deborah worked in many IT corporations in IT, sales and marketing, and human resources before embarking on her holistic therapy career.

She lives in Hampshire (UK) with her husband and cats. She enjoys being close to the sea and the forest. She continues to run her online talk therapy business specialising in trauma.

CONTACT DEBORAH

Wishing you every success in your therapy business. Please do get in touch if you have any questions or would like to share your own experiences.

With love and light, Deborah.

Thank you for purchasing this book. I hope you have enjoyed reading it, please leave a glowing review on Amazon! Here's the link:

https://www.amazon.co.uk/Secret-Being-Good-Therapist-yourself/dp/1728823854

Thank you.

You can contact and connect with me here:

Email

deborah@thespiritwithin.co.uk

Website

https://www.thespiritwithin.co.uk

Facebook

https://www.facebook.com/deborah.thespiritwithin

https://www.facebook.com/thespiritwithintherapy

Twitter

https://www.twitter.com/TSWHypnotherapy

LinkedIn

https://www.linkedin.com/in/deborahbaxter

Instagram

https://www.instagram.com/thespiritwithintherapy/

Printed by Amazon Italia Logistica S.r.l.
Torrazza Piemonte (TO), Italy